Historic Cocktails

by
Dawn Irion

Copyright © 2016 by Dawn Irion

Published by Cat In Hat Books
PO Box 879
Vonore, TN 37885

All rights reserved.

Table of Contents

INTRODUCTION		9
GLOSSARY		13
STEMWARE		19
SIDEKICKS – Additives, Bitters and Liqueurs		21
COCKTAIL RECIPES		27
1.	Abricontine Pousse Café	27
2.	Absinthe	27
3.	Absinthe Cocktail	28
4.	Absinthe Frappe	29
5.	Absinthe, American Service	30
6.	Absinthe, French Service	30
7.	Absinthe, Italian Service	30
8.	Admiral Schley High Ball	30
9.	Ale Sangaree	31
10.	All Right Cocktail	32
11.	American Pousse Cafe	32
12.	Applejack Cocktail	33
13.	Applejack Fix	33
14.	Applejack Sour	34
15.	"Arf-And-Arf"	34
16.	Arrack Punch	34
17.	Astringent	35
18.	Bacardi Cocktail	36
19.	Bacardi Cocktail (Country Club Style)	36
20.	Baldy Cocktail	37
21.	Bamboo Cocktail	38
22.	Benedictine	39
23.	Bishop	39
24.	Bishop A La Prusse	39

25.	Bizzy Izzy High Ball	40
26.	Black Stripe	41
27.	Blackthorne Cocktail	42
28.	Blackthorne Sour	42
29.	Bliz's Royal Rickey	43
30.	Blood Hound Cocktail	44
31.	Blue Blazer	44
32.	Boating Punch	45
33.	Bon Soir ("Good Night")	45
34.	Bottle of Cocktail	46
35.	Brandy and Ginger Ale	47
36.	Brandy and Soda	47
37.	Brandy Float	48
38.	Brandy Julep	48
39.	Brandy Punch	48
40.	Brandy Scaffa	49
41.	Brandy Shake	49
42.	Brandy Skin	50
43.	Brandy Sling	50
44.	Brandy Smash	51
45.	Brandy Sour	52
46.	Brandy Toddy	52
47.	Bronx Cocktail	52
48.	Burnt Brandy	53
49.	Buster Brown Cocktail	54
50.	Buttered Rum	55
51.	California Sherry Cobbler	55
52.	California Wine Cobbler	56
53.	Carleton Rickey (St. Louis Style)	57
54.	Catawba Cobbler	57
55.	Celery Sour	58
56.	Champagne	59
57.	Champagne Cobbler	60
58.	Champagne Cocktail	60
59.	Champagne Frappe	61
60.	Champagne Julep	61
61.	Champagne Sour	62

62.	Champagne Velvet	62
63.	Claret and Ice	63
64.	Claret Cobbler	63
65.	Claret Punch	64
66.	Club Cocktail	64
67.	Club House Claret Punch	65
68.	Cohasset Punch	65
69.	Columbia Skin	66
70.	Continental Sour	66
71.	Cooperstown Cocktail	67
72.	Cordial Lemonade	67
73.	Couperee	68
74.	Creme De Menthe	68
75.	Curacoa	69
76.	Curacoa Punch	70
77.	Currant Shrub	70
78.	Delusion	71
79.	Deronda Cocktail	71
80.	Diarrhea Draught	73
81.	Dixie Cocktail	74
82.	Doray Sour	74
83.	Duplex Cocktail	74
84.	Durkee Cocktail	75
85.	Eagle Punch	76
86.	East India Cocktail	76
87.	El Dorado Punch	77
88.	English Bishop Punch	77
89.	Fancy Whiskey Smash	78
90.	Fedora	79
91.	Fog Horn—Country Club Style	79
92.	French Pousse Café	81
93.	Gibson Cocktail	81
94.	Gillette Cocktail—Chicago Style	82
95.	Gin and Calamus	82
96.	Gin Daisy	84
97.	Gin Sour—Country Club Style	84
98.	Gin Squash—Country Club Style	85

99.	Horse Thief Cocktail	86
100.	Irish Rose	86
101.	Jersey Lightning Cocktail	87
102.	Knabenschue	87
103.	L.P.W.	88
104.	Leaping Frog	89
105.	Lone Tree Cocktail	89
106.	Mint Julep—Kentucky Style	90
107.	Ojen Cocktail	91
108.	Old Fashion Cocktail	91
109.	Onion Cocktail	92
110.	Overall Julep—St. Louis Style	92
111.	Pequot Semer	93
112.	Polo Players' Delight	93
113.	Pousse Cafe—St. Louis	94
114.	Remsen Cooler	95
115.	September Morn Cocktail	97
116.	Shandy Gaff	97
117.	Sherry and Bitters	97
118.	Stinger	98
119.	Stone Sour	99
120.	Tom Tom	99
121.	Twilight Cocktail	100
122.	Whiskey - Scotch Hot	101
123.	Whiskey - Irish Hot	101
124.	Whiskey Punch - St. Louis Style	102

COCKTAIL RECIPES WITH EGG — 103

1.	Ale Flip	104
2.	Bismarck	104
3.	Brace Up	105
4.	Brandy Flip	105
5.	Chocolate Punch	106
6.	Claret Flip	108
7.	Clover Club Cocktail	108
8.	Clover Leaf Cocktail	109
9.	Coffee Cocktail	110
10.	Country Cocktail	110

11.	Dream		111
12.	Doray Punch		111
13.	Egg Milk Punch		112
14.	Eggnog		112
15.	Fannie Ward		113
16.	Free Love Cocktail—Club Style		113
17.	Ramos Gin Fizz		114
18.	Tom and Jerry		115

NON-ALCOHOLIC COCKTAIL RECIPES — 117

1.	Apollinaris Lemonade	117
2.	Auditorium Cooler	117
3.	Beef Tea	118
4.	Black Cow	119
5.	Boston Cooler	120
6.	G.O.P.	121
7.	Golfer's Delight	122
8.	Lemonade Apollinaris	123
9.	Samton Cocktail	123

NON-ALCOHOLIC COCKTAIL RECIPES with EGG — 125

1.	Bombay Cocktail	125
2.	Cider Eggnog	126
3.	Egg Sour	127

PUNCH RECIPES — 129

1.	Black And Tan Punch (For party of 10)	129
2.	Bombay Punch (2½-gallon mixture for 40 people)	130
3.	Brandy Shrub (2-gallon mixture for 40 people)	131
4.	Century Club Punch (for a party of 5)	132
5.	Champagne Cup (makes 2 gallons)	132
6.	Champagne Punch (party of 6)	134
7.	Claret Cup (makes 2 gallons)	134
8.	Claret Punch (makes 5 gallons)	135
9.	Club House Punch (party of 20)	136
10.	Cold Ruby Punch (makes 2½ gallons)	137
11.	Companion Punch (makes 2½ gallons)	137
12.	Country Club Punch	138
13.	Crimean Cup A La Marmora (for a party of 10)	140

14.	Eggnog (makes 3 gallons)	141
15.	Fish Club Punch (for a party of 8)	141
16.	Garden Punch (2½ gallon mixture for a party of 50)	142
17.	Ladies' Delight	143
18.	Pineapple Julep (for a party of 6)	144
19.	Punch A La Romaine (for a party of 16)	145
20.	Tokay Punch (uses 6 pounds of Tokay grapes)	147

Introduction

Nearly 100 years ago, the United States entered a dark period of time called Prohibition. In 1920, the 18th Amendment to the Constitution went into effect, making the manufacture, distribution and sale of intoxicating liquors illegal. It was not illegal to drink alcohol, but it was illegal to make, move or sell it. The reasons behind Prohibition may be summed up by its title "The Noble Experiment". Essentially those who were anti-alcohol were successful in demonizing liquor and promising a glorious society if it would simply ban alcohol. In the 13 years of Prohibition, just the opposite occurred. Jobs were lost, companies went out of business, restaurants closed down and crime increased. Over 10,000 deaths could be attributed directly to tainted, bootlegged, moonshine liquor. In addition to these effects, we nearly lost the great art of both liqueur making and drink mixing. Prior to Prohibition, there were thousands of small distilleries making specialty liqueurs, beers and wines. After Prohibition, there were less than 100 breweries in

America. The only wineries to survive were those who received special dispensation to make alcohol for religious purposes. It took decades for the art of distilling specialized spirits to return to America. For example, it was not until the late 20th century that the United States was again known for making artisan beers.

Pre-prohibition there was also a great deal of interest in mixed drinks and concocting new cocktails. Recipes were crafted both in city and country clubs and those which were judged excellent by customers were passed around by word of mouth. Eventually the best cocktail recipes made it into the bartender's guides of the time. By studying these recipes we can see how many ingredients, which once were common, became lost or nearly lost. Recently there has been renewed interest in many of these old liqueurs and some companies are creating them again. With this revived passion for crafting cocktails, it seemed fitting to study some pre-prohibition recipes and bring them to the fore once again. In this book are nearly 200 recipes judged worthy to be in bartender's guides in the early 1900's. Many of the recipes are non-alcoholic, many are for dinner or larger parties and many call for some specialty ingredients that you may never have heard of before. So take your time, craft a cocktail or two, and relive the glory days of the cocktail.

Prohibition Quick Facts

- Prohibition began with the passage of the 18th Amendment, ratified on January 16, 1919, and went into effect on January 17, 1920.

- Prohibition ended with the passage of the 21st Amendment, ratified on December 5, 1933, which was effective on December 15, 1933.

- The Volstead Act, passed October 27, 1919, empowered the States to enforce Prohibition, but not every state policed the ban. Maryland was the most fervent anti-Prohibition state and refused to allocate any police resources to enforce Prohibition.

- There were several loop-holes to the 18th Amendment, among them alcohol for pharmaceutical uses. Walgreens can thank Prohibition for growing from about 20 locations to more than 500 during the 1920s.

- Some states retained the ban on alcohol after the passage of the 21st Amendment. Mississippi was the last to relent in 1966, however to this day 10 states still have "dry" counties where alcohol sales are prohibited.

Glossary

Aperitif – an alcoholic beverage consumed before a meal as an appetizer.

Bar Spoon – a long mixing spoon which may have a lemon zester or similar tool on the other end.

Bitters – alcohol infused with botanicals, such as herbs and roots, yielding a spirit with a bitter, sour, or bittersweet flavor. Many bitters were originally developed for medicinal purposes, but are now used as digestifs or cocktail flavorings.

Dash – a flick of the wrist to put a very small amount, about 1/32 fl. ounce or 1 mL into a beverage.

Digestif – an alcoholic beverage consumed during or after a meal to aid digestion. Common digestifs are Brandy, fruit brandies, fortified wines, liqueurs and liquor cocktails.

Drachm (drachma, dram) - an eighth of an ounce.

Cocktail – now generally understood to mean any mixed drink, but was originally defined as a beverage containing spirits, sugar, water and bitters.

Float – when one alcohol sits atop another alcohol in a glass without mixing. Instructions will call for the heaviest liqueur or cordial to be poured first. Subsequent liqueurs can be poured very carefully down the side of the glass or poured over an inverted spoon, allowing the alcohol to trickle off the spoon in many directions, or to be laid on with a spoon from another glass.

FLOATED INCORRECTLY   FLOATED CORRECTLY

Gill – equals 4 fluid ounces in the United States or a quarter of a pint or 118 ml.

Highball – Any liqueur mixed with soda, served in a tall glass (the glass itself is often called a highball).

Jigger – 1 1/2 fluid ounces, or 45 ml or 4.5 cl. A jigger can also refer to the double barreled bartender's tool itself.

Liquor – an alcohol distilled from grains or plants, such as rum, vodka or whiskey and considered by some as a synonym for "spirit".

Liqueur – a sweet, flavored grain based alcohol made with fruit, herbs, flowers, nuts and/or spices plus sugar.

Muddler – a wooden pestle used to crush ("muddle") fruit in a glass. Typically used in the preparation of Mojito, Caipirinha and Old Fashioned cocktails. Modern muddlers may be may of stainless steel alone or stainless steel with a rubber end.

Pony or Pony Shot – 1 fluid ounce, or 30 ml or 3 cl.

Shake – To add ingredients, including ice, into the serving glass, then pour everything into a shaker tin and shake. Pour everything back into the original glass.

Splash – About 1/12 fl ounce or 2-3 mL, but can be as generous as the bartender would like.

Strain – To drain the liquid out of a shaker tin through a Strainer.

Tools – Essential bar tools include a cocktail shaker, a jigger, a hawthorne strainer and ice tongs. Optional tools would include a bar spoon, a julep strainer, a muddler, a speed pourer and garnishing tools.

Ice Terms

The following recipes will call for various forms of ice in order to present the beverage with the best appearance and flavor.

Cubes – can vary in size from what is produced by a home ice maker to large lump ice. The larger the ice, the slower it melts and the less it dilutes the cocktail. One might also use a custom "ice ball" maker for presentation as may be seen at a local drinkery.

Cracked ice is like a small ice cube, it will melt somewhat to help dilute strong cocktails.

Crushed ice, also known as fine ice, is broken up ice cubes. Very strong drinks are often served with ice crushed to dilute the beverage as it is consumed.

Shaved or "snow" ice is as it sounds, the consistency of snow.

Block ice would be large blocks of ice used in punch recipes, which melt slowly and thus do not dilute the punch.

Stemware

You will find that this book of recipes has suggestions for the preferred glass in which to serve your creations. While owning every variety of stemware is not required in order to give your guests an excellent cocktail experience, this guide is provided as a reference should you choose to serve the drinks as suggested.

Sidekicks
Additives, Bitters and Liqueurs

(Several of these ingredients are covered in more detail throughout the book.)

Angelica wine – A sweet dessert wine, typically made from the "mission" grape brought to the new world with Spanish missionaries.

Angostura Bitters – A concentrated, botanically infused alcoholic mixture of water, ethanol, gentian, herbs and spices. Named for the town of Angostura (now Ciudad Bolívar) in Venezuela where the bitters were developed. Used in small amounts as flavoring.

Anisette – A liqueur flavored by the sweet and fragrant herb anise.

Benedictine – A 86 proof liqueur crafted from 27 or 28 different botanicals. The exact recipe and process are a secret, but includes

distillation through copper stills and aging in oak barrels. The liqueur's primary ingredients are angelica, hyssop and lemon balm. Other plants and spices may include vanilla, myrrh, nutmeg, mace, cloves, cinnamon, cardamom and saffron. The name is rumored to come from the liqueur's development by a Benedictine monk.

Burgundy – Generic for unblended wines from Burgundy, France but has become synonymous with unblended wines produced in other places. Can refer to either white or red, but if not specified, it would mean red. May substitute with any wine of the specified color.

Chartreuse – Brand name for a 110 proof herbal based bitters, green as its name implies. Also available as a 142 proof elixir.

Cordial – An alcoholic beverage with at least 2.5% sugar content. In some areas of the world the term is interchangeable with the term "liqueur." Most cordials begin as a neutral grain alcohol and are infused with flavors from herbs, fruit, nuts and/or spices. Cordials are often an ingredient in mixed drinks but may also be enjoyed alone over ice. Cordials have a low alcohol content between 15-30% and are not aged.

Curacoa (Curacao) – Orange flavored liqueur, can be of a variety of food colors without affecting flavor.

Grenadine (Cusenier Grenadine) – Non-alcoholic, pomegranate syrup. Best to avoid those made from artificial flavorings. May substitute with red currant or raspberry syrup.

Gum syrup - A rich simple syrup (2 sugar to 1 water) combined with gum, Arabic resin, harvested from the Acacia tree. Acts as an emulsifier so that all the components of the beverage are uniformly blended. Gum syrup is a favored tool of the best bartenders to elevate the texture and weight of cocktails. Available in specialty stores and online.

Jamaica Ginger – Liquid extract of the ginger root.

Maraschino – A clear, cherry flavored liqueur.

Orange bitters – A concentrated liquid spirit with extractions of orange peel, spices and herbs. May substitute with some orange peel macerated in Angostura.

Orgeat Syrup – A syrup made of almonds, orange flower water and sometimes barley water. Non-alcoholic flavoring used in cocktails.

Can be clear or milky golden in color. May substitute with any almond syrup.

Port – also known as Porto. Generic for a spiced, sweet and rich aged Portuguese wine.

Sherry Wine – Also known as dry sherry, generic for a Spanish fortified wine. May substitute with Dry Sack or other cocktail Sherry.

Tokay – A sweet white wine.

Tuaca – The brand name for an Italian, vanilla flavored liqueur. Substitutes include Cuarente y Tres, creme de vanilla or sweetened vanilla-flavored vodka.

Vanilla Cordial – An extract of vanilla made from vanilla beans, vodka, sugar and water. May substitute with Tuaca or sweet vanilla flavored vodka.

Cocktail Recipes

1. ABRICOTINE POUSSE CAFE

Fill Pousse Café (or similar) glass one-third full of Abricotine and add Maraschino, Curacoa, Chartreuse and Brandy in equal proportions until the glass is filled. The ingredients should be poured in one after the other from a small Wine glass, with great care, to prevent the colors from blending. Ignite the Brandy on top, and after it has blazed for a few seconds extinguishing it by placing a saucer or the bottom of another glass over the blazing fluid. Then serve.

ABRICOTINE is a French brand of apricot flavored brandy. Allowed substitutions are any apricot brandy or apricot liqueur.

2. ABSINTHE

To serve Absinthe without any particular style of service:

Fill the bowl of the Absinthe glass partly with Shaved Ice, and the rest with water, the water will be ice cold as it drops from the Absinthe glass. Pour one pony of Absinthe into large Bar glass and let ice cold water drip from the Absinthe glass into Bar glass until full. The Absinthe glass has a hole in the center.

ABSINTHE is a distilled 90-148 proof alcoholic beverage derived from botanicals, including the flowers and leaves of Artemisia absinthium ("grand wormwood"). The anise-flavored spirit can include green anise, sweet fennel, and other medicinal and culinary herbs. Absinthe is traditionally a natural green in color but it may also be colorless. In historical literature Absinthe has been referred to as "la fée verte" (the green fairy). Absinthe originated in the canton of Neuchâtel in Switzerland in the late 18th century. Today, Switzerland is the only country to have a legal standard for the production of Absinthe. Absinthe quickly rose to great popularity as an alcoholic drink in late 19th- and early 20th-century, however it gained a false and hysterical reputation for producing hallucinations. Trace amounts of the chemical compound thujone were alleged to cause harmful effects. However no substantial evidence exists to support these claims. In the 1990's, modern European Union food and beverage laws were adopted which removed the longstanding barriers to the production and sale of Absinthe. A revived interest in the spirit followed. Now nearly 200 brands of absinthe are being produced in a dozen countries, primarily in France, Switzerland, Australia, Spain, and the Czech Republic. It wasn"t until 2007 that U.S. producers were approved for distilling and distributing Absinthe.

3. ABSINTHE COCKTAIL

Mixing glass ¾ full Shaved Ice.

½ jigger Water.

½ jigger Absinthe.

2 dashes Angostura Bitters.

1 teaspoonful Benedictine.

Stir; strain into Cocktail glass and serve.

4. ABSINTHE FRAPPE

Fill medium Bar glass full of Shaved Ice.

1 teaspoonful Benedictine.

1 pony Absinthe.

Shake until outside of Shaker has frosty appearance; strain into six-ounce Shell glass and serve.

5. ABSINTHE, AMERICAN SERVICE

Mixing glass ¾ full Shaved Ice.

4 dashes Gum Syrup.

1 pony Absinthe.

Shake until outside of shaker is well frosted; strain into large Champagne glass and serve.

6. ABSINTHE, FRENCH SERVICE

Fill the bowl of your Absinthe glass with Shaved Ice and water. Raise the bowl and let the Ice Water drip into 1 pony of Absinthe until the proper color is obtained. Serve in thin Bar glass.

7. ABSINTHE, ITALIAN SERVICE

In a large Bar glass:

1 pony of Absinthe

3 pieces Cracked Ice

3 dashes Maraschino

½ pony Anisette

Add ice water while stirring gently with Bar Spoon. Serve.

8. ADMIRAL SCHLEY HIGH BALL

Drop a piece of Ice into a High Ball glass.

1 teaspoonful Pineapple Syrup.

1 teaspoonful Lemon Juice.

2/3 jigger Irish Whiskey.

2/3 jigger Tokay, Angelica or Sweet Catawba Wine.

Fill up with Apollinaris or Seltzer.

APOLLINARIS, "The Queen of Table Waters", is a brand name for a naturally sparkling mineral water from a spring in Germany.

---

9. ALE SANGAREE

Dissolve in an Ale glass 1 teaspoonful Bar Sugar.

Fill up with Ale and serve with grated Nutmeg on top.

ALE is made of fermented malted barley and water, usually without hops. Malted barley is made by allowing the barley grain to partially sprout before being dried. The grain is soaked in water for about 40 hours, then drained and held at about 60° F until it starts to sprout, about 5 days. The barley is slowly dried in a kiln at temperatures gradually rising to 122 F for lighter malts and 220 F for darker malts. This kiln drying takes about 30 hours. The malted barley is then ground to create a "mash" and mixed with water in order to dissolve the starch, sugar and enzymes. The temperature of the "mash" is then raised to 150-160 F. After all the starches are converted to sugars, the mixture is filtered. The sweet liquid that remains is called "malt extract" and is then fermented to become ale. There are several varieties of ale from new to old, from Scotch to Belgian. Examples of new ale would be Pale Ale or brown ales. Old ales (or stock ales) are aged in oak barrels, have more malt and a dark amber color with a more mellowed flavor. Brewing Ale is an art, just as mixing a good drink, so you may want to visit a local tasting room to be sure you like your ale before trying the following recipes.

10. ALL RIGHT COCKTAIL

Use a large Mixing glass filled with Lump Ice.

1 jigger Rye Whiskey.

2/3 jigger Orange Curacoa.

1 dash Angostura Bitters.

Shake well; strain into Cocktail glass and serve.

◇◇◇◇◇◇◇◇◇◇◇◇◇◇◇◇◇◇◇◇◇◇◇◇◇◇◇◇◇◇◇

RYE WHISKEY – a single-malt whiskey distilled from mostly rye mash, which may be combined with corn mash. Is mainly an American whiskey, produced historically in Pennsylvania. The flavor profile is similar to Bourbon but is drier and not as sweet with tones of grain, tannin and oak.

◇◇◇◇◇◇◇◇◇◇◇◇◇◇◇◇◇◇◇◇◇◇◇◇◇◇◇◇◇◇◇

11. AMERICAN POUSSE CAFE

Fill a Pousse Cafe glass ¼ full of Chartreuse, and add Maraschino, Curacoa and Brandy in equal proportions until the glass is filled.

Then proceed as for Abricotine Pousse Cafe. Ignite the Brandy on top, and after it has blazed for a few seconds extinguishing it by placing a saucer or the bottom of another glass over the blazing fluid. Then serve.

12. APPLE JACK COCKTAIL

Fill large Bar glass ¾ full Shaved Ice.

3 dashes Gum Syrup.

3 dashes Raspberry Syrup.

1¼ jiggers Applejack.

Shake; strain into Cocktail glass and serve with piece of Lemon Peel twisted on top.

APPLEJACK (Apple Jack Brandy) was the first distilled spirit in the New World. It gets its name from "jacking" - freeze distillation where the fermented apple cider was allowed to freeze outside, then the ice was removed. This process concentrated the flavor as well as the alcohol content. Any variety of apple brandy may be used as a substitute.

13. APPLEJACK FIX

Fill large Bar glass with Shaved Ice.

2 teaspoonfuls Bar Sugar dissolved in little water.

¼ Juice of 1 Lemon.

3 dashes of Curacoa.

4 dashes of any Fruit Syrup.

1 jigger Applejack Brandy.

Stir; dress with Fruits; serve with Straws.

14. APPLEJACK SOUR

Fill large Bar glass ¾ full Shaved Ice.

2 teaspoonfuls Bar Sugar dissolved in little water.

3 dashes lemon or Lime Juice.

1 jigger Applejack.

Stir well; strain into Sauer glass; dress with Fruit and Berries and serve.

15. ARF-AND-ARF

Pour into an Ale glass, or mug, ½ Porter and ½ Ale

or Porter and Stout with Ale

or ½ Old and ½ New Ale.

The use of the Porter and Ale was more prevalent in England. In the United States ½ Old and ½ New Ale was the usual.

16. ARRACK PUNCH

Pour into a Punch glass the Juice of 1 Lime and a little Apollinaris water in which a heaping teaspoonful of Bar Sugar has been dissolved.

Add:

1 Lump Ice.

¾ jigger Batavia Arrack.

¼ Jigger Jamaica Rum.

Stir well; dash with Champagne; stir again briskly; dress with Fruit and Serve.

◇◇

BATAVIA ARRACK (Arak) is a spirit distilled from fermented sugarcane & Javanese rice. It originated in modern day Jakarta, Indonesia. May use white rum as a substitution.

◇◇

17. ASTRINGENT

½ wineglass Port Wine.

6 dashes Jamaica Ginger.

Fill up with Brandy

Stir gently and serve with little Nutmeg on top.

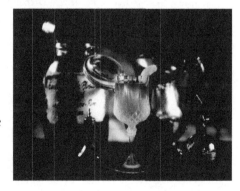

◇◇

BRANDY usually refers to spirits made from distilling wine or fermented grape juice. However brandy can be generic for any spirit distilled from fruits, such as applejack mentioned above. Other well known names for brandy are Cognac and Armagnac named for those regions in France.

◇◇

18. BACARDI COCKTAIL

Use a large Mixing glass.

Fill with Lump Ice.

½ jigger Grenadine.

1 jigger Bacardi Rum.

Shake well and serve in a Cocktail glass.

BACARDI RUM was first distilled in Cuba in 1862. During Prohibition, Cuba was popular with US tourists and Barcardi used this opportunity to successfully brand Cuba as the "home of rum" and Bacardi as the "king of rums." After Prohibition, Barcardi moved much of its operations to Puerto Rico, which fortuitously saved the company from Castro's plans to nationalize it in the 1960's. Despite the loss of all assets left behind in Cuba, Barcardi was able to build the company from its base in Puerto Rico to become the most well known and sold rum in the world.

19. BACARDI COCKTAIL
Country Club Style

Use a large Mixing glass

Fill with Lump Ice.

½ Lime Juice.

2 dashes Imported Grenadine.

1 jigger Bacardi Rum.

Shake well; strain into Cocktail glass and serve.

◇◇◇◇◇◇◇◇◇◇◇◇◇◇◇◇◇◇◇◇◇◇◇◇◇◇◇◇◇◇◇◇◇◇◇◇

This modern version of the Bacardi cocktail is modeled after the Country Club Style of the original Bacardi cocktail.

◇◇◇◇◇◇◇◇◇◇◇◇◇◇◇◇◇◇◇◇◇◇◇◇◇◇◇◇◇◇◇◇◇◇◇◇

20. BALDY COCKTAIL

Use a large Mixing glass with Lump Ice.

1 jigger of Burnette's Old Tom Gin.//
1 pony of Orange Juice.//
1 Dash of Orange Bitters.

Shake; strain into Cocktail glass and serve.

◇◇◇◇◇◇◇◇◇◇◇◇◇◇◇◇◇◇◇◇◇◇◇◇◇◇◇◇◇◇◇◇◇◇◇◇

BURNETTE'S OLD TOM GIN – brand name for a London based Gin maker of the 19th century. May substitute with any Tom gin or juniper flavored gin, though the later may need to be sweetened.

◇◇◇◇◇◇◇◇◇◇◇◇◇◇◇◇◇◇◇◇◇◇◇◇◇◇◇◇◇◇◇◇◇◇◇◇

21. BAMBOO COCKTAIL

Fill large Bar glass 1/3 full Fine Ice.

¾ Sherry Wine.

¾ Italian Vermouth.

Stir; strain into Cocktail glass. Serve.

◇◇◇◇◇◇◇◇◇◇◇◇◇◇◇◇◇◇◇◇◇◇◇◇◇◇◇◇◇◇◇◇◇◇◇◇

ITALIAN VERMOUTH is also known as rosso vermouth or red vermouth. It is a sweet, red colored, spiced wine which is actually made from white wine. May substitute with any red aperitif wine.

◇◇◇◇◇◇◇◇◇◇◇◇◇◇◇◇◇◇◇◇◇◇◇◇◇◇◇◇◇◇◇◇◇◇◇◇

22. BENEDICTINE

Place an inverted Whiskey glass on the bar, set a Pony glass on it and fill up with Benedictine. Serve straight.

23. BISHOP

1 teaspoonful Bar Sugar in large Bar glass.

2 dashes Lemon Juice with the Skin of Two Slices.

Fill glass ¾ full Shaved Ice.

1 dash Seltzer Water.

2 dashes Jamaica Rum.

Fill up with Claret or Burgundy; shake; ornament with Fruit and serve with Straws.

Unlike Barcardi rum, JAMAICA RUM is dark, sweeter and richer. Dark rums, like Jamaican, are typically aged in charred oak barrels and aged longer. Caramel may be added. White rum is usually aged in stainless steel barrels for less time and is filtered.

24. BISHOP A LA PRUSSE

Halve 6 large Oranges and broil in the oven until they are of a light brown color, about 10 minutes. Watch to avoid burning. Place the oranges in a deep dish, scatter with ½ lb. of sugar and pour on 1 pint of Port or

Claret Wine. Cover the dish and set aside for 24 hours before the time to serve. When about ready to serve, warm the entire dish in boiling water. Press the Juice from the Oranges with a large spoon or wooden potato masher, then strain the Juice through a fine sieve or cheese cloth. Boil 1 pint of Port or Claret and mix it with the Strained Juice. Serve in stem Claret glasses while warm. A little Nutmeg on top improves the drink, but should not be added unless requested by your guest.

25. BIZZY IZZY HIGH BALL

Drop 1 piece of Ice into a Highball glass.

2 dashes Lemon Juice.

2 teaspoonfuls Pineapple Syrup.

½ jigger Sherry Wine.

½ jigger Rye or Bourbon Whiskey.

BOURBON WHISKEY is a single-malt whiskey distilled from primarily corn mash which may also have some wheat or rye grains. Has the flavor of grain, tannin and oak. May substitute with rye whiskey.

26. BLACK STRIPE

In a small Bar glass add:

Santa Cruz or Jamaica Rum

1 tablespoonful of Molasses

If serving hot, fill glass with boiling water and sprinkle Nutmeg on top.

If serving cold, add ½ wineglass water. Stir well and fill up with Shaved Ice.

◇◇

SANTA CRUZ RUM is a lighter sugar cane and molasses-based spirit from the Virgin Islands. Use any light rum.

◇◇

27. BLACKTHORNE COCKTAIL

Fill Mixing glass 2/3 full Shaved Ice.

¼ teaspoonful Lemon Juice.

1 teaspoonful Syrup.

½ jigger Vermouth.

½ jigger Sloe Gin.

1 dash Angostura Bitters.

2 dashes Orange Bitters.

Stir; strain into Cocktail glass and serve.

◇◇

SLOE GIN is a fruit flavored liqueur made from the "sloeberry" or "blackthorn plum"" fruit of a shrub native to Northern Europe. May substitute with other plum, prune or berry flavored liqueurs.

◇◇

28. BLACKTHORNE SOUR

Fill large Bar glass 2/3 full Shaved Ice.

4 dashes Lime or Lemon Juice.

1 teaspoonful Pineapple Syrup.

½ teaspoonful green Chartreuse.

1 jigger Sloe Gin.

Stir; strain into Claret glass; ornament with Fruit and serve.

29. BLIZ'S ROYAL RICKEY

Drop 3 lumps Cracked Ice in a Rickey (thin Champagne) glass.

½ Lime or ¼ Lemon.

4 dashes Raspberry Syrup.

1 pony Vermouth.

¾ jigger Gin.

Fill up with Ginger Ale (imported); stir; dress with Fruit and serve.

◇◇◇◇◇◇◇◇◇◇◇◇◇◇◇◇◇◇◇◇◇◇◇◇◇◇◇◇◇◇◇◇◇◇◇◇

When the variety of GIN is unspecified, it generally is calling for a dry gin, like London Dry Gin. May also substitute with vodka, schnapps, other neutral spirit.

◇◇◇◇◇◇◇◇◇◇◇◇◇◇◇◇◇◇◇◇◇◇◇◇◇◇◇◇◇◇◇◇◇◇◇◇

30. BLOOD HOUND COCKTAIL

Fill large Bar glass ½ full Shaved Ice.

Add ½ dozen fresh Strawberries.

1 jigger Burnette's Old Tom Gin.

Shake well; strain into Cocktail glass and serve.

31. BLUE BLAZER

Use two Pewter or Silver Mugs.

1 teaspoonful Bar Sugar dissolved in a little Hot Water.
1 jigger of Scotch Whiskey.

Ignite the mixture, and while blazing pour it several times from one mug to the other. Serve with a piece of twisted Lemon Peel on top.

◇◇◇◇◇◇◇◇◇◇◇◇◇◇◇◇◇◇◇◇◇◇◇◇◇◇◇◇◇◇◇◇◇◇◇◇◇

SCOTCH WHISKEY, or simply Scotch, is a malt whiskey made in Scotland. The first known mention of Scotch whiskey was in 1495 by a friar named John Cor, who distilled the spirit at Lindores Abbey. Originally, all Scotch was made from malted barley, but wheat and rye were introduced in the late 18th century. There are five distinct categories of the whiskey: single malt, single grain, blended malt, blended grain and blended Scotch whiskey. It is aged in oak barrels for at least three years. Blended Scotch whiskey is acceptable for use in cocktails whereas a higher grade would be desired for drinking straight to enjoy its oakey and smoky flavor. The term dram refers to a single unit for drinking.

◇◇◇◇◇◇◇◇◇◇◇◇◇◇◇◇◇◇◇◇◇◇◇◇◇◇◇◇◇◇◇◇◇◇◇◇◇

32. BOATING PUNCH

Into a large Bar glass put:

2 teaspoonfuls Bar Sugar.

2 dashes Lemon Juice.

1 dash Lime Juice.

Fill up with Shaved Ice and add:

1 pony Brandy.

1 jigger Santa Cruz rum.

Stir; dress with Fruit and serve with Straws.

33. BON SOIR
("Good Night")

Fill a Sherry glass ½ full of Shaved Ice.

½ pony Benedictine.

½ pony Creme Yvette.

Fill up with Ginger Ale; stir gently and serve with a Straw cut in two.

◇◇◇

CRÈME YVETTE is the brand name for a liqueur infused with the flavor from Violet petals which is no longer available. There is a substitute, liqueur de violette, but it is rare in the United States. Recommended substitutes available in the U.S. would be a liqueur with a vanilla, citrus and spiced flavor such as Tuaca.

◇◇◇

34. BOTTLE OF COCKTAIL

Pour a quart of Whiskey or other desired liqueur into a glass pitcher and add:

1 jigger Gum Syrup.

1 pony Curacoa.

¾ pony Angostura Bitters.

Pour back and forth from one pitcher into another until the liquid is thoroughly mixed. Bottle and cork. Save and serve on demand over ice.

35. BRANDY AND GINGER ALE

3 cubes of Ice in tall, thin glass.

1 wineglass Brandy.
1 bottle Ginger Ale.
Stir briskly and serve.

36. BRANDY AND SODA

2 pieces of Ice in tall, thin glass.

1 wineglass Brandy.
1 bottle plain Soda.
Stir briskly and serve.

37. BRANDY FLOAT

Fill a Cocktail glass 2/3 full of Carbonated Water.

Use a spoon to float 1 pony of the Brandy on the top.

―――――――――――――――――――

Some of these recipes not only test your taste buds but also your dexterity!

―――――――――――――――――――

38. BRANDY JULEP

Into a small Bar glass pour ¾ wineglass of water and stir in 1 heaping teaspoonful of Bar Sugar. Bruise 3 or 4 sprigs of Mint in the Sugar and Water with a Muddler until the flavor of the Mint has been extracted. Fill a tall Shell glass or large Goblet with fine ice. Strain the mint flavored water just prepared over the ice.

Add:

1 jigger of Brandy.

2 dashes Jamaica Rum.

Stir well. Decorate with a few sprigs of Mint by planting the sprigs stems downward in the Ice around the rim of glass, if desired. Dress with Fruit and serve.

39. BRANDY PUNCH

Fill large Bar glass ¾ full Shaved Ice.

2 teaspoonfuls Bar Sugar dissolved in little Water.

½ Juice of 1 Lemon.

¼ jigger Santa Cruz Rum.

1½ jiggers Brandy.

1 slice Orange.

1 piece of Pineapple.

Shake; dress with Fruit and serve with Straw.

40. BRANDY SCAFFA

Into a small Wineglass pour equal amounts of:

Green Chartreuse.

Maraschino.

Old Brandy.

Use care, not allowing the colors to blend.

41. BRANDY SHAKE

Fill small Bar glass ¾ full Shaved Ice.

1 teaspoonful Bar Sugar.

Juice of 2 Limes.

1 jigger Brandy.

Shake; strain into small fancy glass and serve.

42. BRANDY SKIN

Fill a Whiskey glass ½ full Hot Water and pour in:

1 jigger Brandy.

Twist a piece of Lemon Skin on top and serve.

Optional – stir in ½ small teaspoonful of sugar, depending on preference.

43. BRANDY SLING

In a Whiskey glass:

1 lump Ice.

1 teaspoonful Sugar dissolved in little Water.

1 jigger Brandy.

Stir; twist in a piece of Lemon Peel; grate Nutmeg on top and serve.

44. BRANDY SMASH

Fill large Bar glass ½ full with Shaved Ice.

1 heaping teaspoonful Bar Sugar.

3 sprigs of Mint.

1 jigger Brandy.

Stir; strain into fancy Stem glass and serve.

◇◇

A SPRIG OF MINT is a stem of the mint plant with at least 3 mint leaves growing out of it.

◇◇

45. BRANDY SOUR

Fill large Bar glass ¾ full with Shaved Ice.

2 teaspoonfuls Bar Sugar.

3 dashes Lemon or Lime Juice.

3 dashes Seltzer or Apollinaris Water.

1 jigger Brandy.

Stir; strain into Sour glass; dress with Fruit and serve.

46. BRANDY TODDY

Into a Whiskey glass drop 1 lump Cracked Ice.

Add 1 teaspoonful of Bar Sugar dissolved in little Water. Stir.

Serve with the Brandy bottle and allow your guest to pour their own drink.

47. BRONX COCKTAIL

Fill large Bar glass ¾ full with Shaved Ice.

1/3 jigger Dry Gin.

1/3 jigger French Vermouth.

1/3 jigger Italian Vermouth.

1 Slice Orange.

Shake well; strain into Cocktail glass and serve.

◇◇◇

FRENCH VERMOUTH is also known as dry vermouth, white vermouth or blanc vermouth. It is a French, dry, fortified, herbal wine aperitif. Sweet vermouth was first imported to the United States from Italy in the 1870's. Later, the dryer and lighter version was imported from France. May substitute with other light colored aperitif wines.

48. BURNT BRANDY

Place two lumps of Cut Loaf Sugar in a small, shallow dish or saucer and pour over the Sugar 1½ jiggers of Cognac Brandy. Ignite the Sugar and Brandy and let them burn for about two minutes. Then cover the dish or saucer with a plate, and when the fire is extinguished pour the liquid into a small Bar glass and serve.

COGNAC BRANDY is a variety of brandy from the Cognac region of France produced according to a specific standard. In ordered to be considered Cognac, it must be made from grapes of the region, distilled twice in copper pot stills and aged at least two years in French oak barrels. However, most cognacs are aged considerably longer than two years. May substitute with drier, aged brandy.

49. BUSTER BROWN COCKTAIL

Fill large Bar glass 2/3 full Shaved Ice.

1 teaspoonful Gum Syrup.

2 dashes Lemon Juice.

2 dashes Orange Bitters.

1 jigger Whiskey.

Stir; strain into Cocktail glass and serve.

◇◇◇◇◇◇◇◇◇◇◇◇◇◇◇◇◇◇◇◇◇◇◇◇◇◇◇◇◇◇◇◇◇◇◇◇◇◇

WHISKEY is a general terms referring to any grain-based, oak-aged distillate. In the United States there are several varieties such as Bourbon, rye, American straight, American blended and Tennessee whiskey. Canada has Canadian whiskey; Ireland has Irish whiskey, in both blended and single malt; Japan has its various iterations; and Scotland has Scotch whiskey in blended, single malt, and vatted forms. When the recipe does not specify choose a whiskey most desirable for your guests.

◇◇◇◇◇◇◇◇◇◇◇◇◇◇◇◇◇◇◇◇◇◇◇◇◇◇◇◇◇◇◇◇◇◇◇◇◇◇

50. BUTTERED RUM

In a Tumbler drop 1 lump of Sugar and dissolve it in a little hot Water.

Add:

1¼ Jiggers Rum.

1 piece of Butter about the size of a Walnut.

Grate Nutmeg on top and serve.

For best flavor, use raw milk butter, or an all-natural product like Kerrygold.

51. CALIFORNIA SHERRY COBBLER

Fill glass with Shaved Ice, add:

1 pony of Pineapple Syrup in large Bar glass.

2 jiggers California Sherry.

Stir well; decorate with Fruit; dash a little Port Wine on top and serve with Straws.

CALIFORNIA SHERRY is a fortified wine made of blended California grapes. May substitute with any cocktail Sherry.

52. CALIFORNIA WINE COBBLER

Fill tall, thin glass nearly full Shaved Ice.

1 heaping teaspoonful Bar Sugar.

Juice of 1 Orange.

2½ jiggers California Wine.

Stir; ornament with Fruit and serve with Straws.

When these recipes were originally crafted, California wine was considered an inferior wine. California wineries languished in the background for decades until the 1970's when a wine competition put a Napa Valley winery on the map. In the 1973 "Judgment of Paris" a Chateau Montelena Chardonnay defeated the French wines in a blind taste test. The event inspired the recommended and acclaimed 2008 film "Bottle Shock". While there was some creative license, the basic story is true and captured the passion that Gustavo Brambila, the vintner, has for the art of making excellent wines. More about this event is cover at CatInHatBooks.com.

53. CARLETON RICKEY
St. Louis Style

Use a large Mixing glass; fill with lump Ice.

Juice 1 Lime.

Drop squeezed Lime in glass.

1 jigger Old Bourbon Whiskey.

Fill with Sweet Soda.

Stir well and serve.

54. CATAWBA COBBLER

Fill large Bar glass ½ full of Shaved Ice.

1 teaspoonful Bar Sugar dissolved in a little Water.

1½ jiggers Catawba Wine.

¼ slice of Orange.

Stir well; decorate with Berries and serve with Straws.

CATAWBA WINE is a light, fruity, aromatic wine made from the native American red grape "Catawba," grown primarily on the East Coast of the United States. The Catawba grape produces a semi-dry, semi-sweet or sweet variety of wine and is also used in juice, jams and jellies. The Catawba grape is slow to ripen which deepens its flavor profile of floral and mixed fruit. While the grape is red, they don't contain much anthocyanins, so the resulting wine is light pink, or even white. The wine is also low in tannins making it a great choice for those sensitive to tannins.

55. CELERY SOUR

Fill large Bar glass full Shaved Ice.

1 teaspoonful Lemon Juice.

1 teaspoonful Pineapple Syrup.

1 teaspoonful Celery Bitters.

Stir; strain into Fancy Wineglass with Fruit and serve.

CELERY BITTERS was developed in the 19th century as a health tonic and, as we have seen, ingredients which boasted health benefits were frequently included in cocktails. It has a very potent flavor, so be careful to not add too much. The bitter is quite herbaceous and bracing. With Prohibition, celery bitters seemed doomed to obscurity, but with recent renewed interest in the art of making cocktails, the bitter has made a comeback. Three companies now produced it: Fee Brothers, Scrappy's and The Bitter Truth. The later who won the Spirit of the Year Award in 2008 for its celery bitters.

56. CHAMPAGNE

Fill an ice bucket with one-half ice and one-half water and chill the Champagne bottle for 20-30 minutes. Alternatively, you may refrigerate the bottle for 3 to 4 hours.

Serve off the Ice very cold, but do not chill the glass. Ice should never be put in Champagne as it will ruin its taste and smell.

◇◇

CHAMPAGNE is sparkling white wine from the Champagne region of France. The bubbling was originally a non-desirable consequence of fermenting wine in a region that was too cold for the yeast to convert all of the sugars in the first season. Many of the glass bottles were too weak for the building pressure of carbon dioxide gas as the yeast fermented in the warming springtime. Cellars were found with burst bottles and much wine was lost. As late as the 17th century, vintners were still trying to solve the problem of the bubbly. At some point in the 1700's, Philippe II, Duke of Orléans, succeeded in making the sparkling wine a favorite among the royal and wealthy.

Champenois vintners then began to intentionally make their wines bubbly, but still faced the problem of exploding bottles. In the 1800's, glass technology finally developed for champagne to be widely produced in a profitable manner. It was then that Champagne began to be used in cocktail recipes. This popularity was short lived. There was a French vineyard riot in 1910-11 which drastically lowered supply; then the Russian Revolution and American Prohibition drastically lowered demand. The First and Second World Wars nearly decimated the vineyards, which became battlefields. Thankfully, something of the

Champagne vineyards survived and interest renewed in the 1950's to restore the beverage. Today there are 86,500 acres producing over 200 million bottles of Champagne per year.

◇◇◇◇◇◇◇◇◇◇◇◇◇◇◇◇◇◇◇◇◇◇◇◇◇◇◇◇◇◇◇◇◇◇◇◇◇◇

57. CHAMPAGNE COBBLER

Fill Bar glass ½ full with Shaved Ice. Add:

1 teaspoonful Bar Sugar.

1 slice Lemon Peel.

1 slice Orange Peel

Fill up with Champagne.

Decorate with Fruit and serve with Straws.

58. CHAMPAGNE COCKTAIL

1 small piece Ice in a thin glass. Add:

1 lump Sugar in tall

2 dashes Angostura Bitters.

1 piece twisted Lemon Peel.

Fill up with Champagne.

Stir and serve.

◇◇◇◇◇◇◇◇◇◇◇◇◇◇◇◇◇◇◇◇◇◇◇◇◇◇◇◇◇◇◇◇◇◇◇◇◇◇

This modern Champagne Cocktail does not call for a small piece of ice or orange peel, however does call for a small amount of Cognac. Amount of Angostura Bitters is the same.

◇◇◇◇◇◇◇◇◇◇◇◇◇◇◇◇◇◇◇◇◇◇◇◇◇◇◇◇◇◇◇◇◇◇◇◇◇◇

59. CHAMPAGNE FRAPPE

Place a chilled bottle of Champagne in a bucket and surround it with equal amounts of fine Ice and Salt. Twirl the bottle until it is about to freeze, about 2 hours. Don't allow to completely freeze. When served it will have a slushy consistency.

60. CHAMPAGNE JULEP

Fill medium size Shell glass 1/3 full Cracked Ice.

2 teaspoonfuls Bar Sugar.

2 sprigs bruised Mint.

Pour Champagne slowly into the glass, stirring gently at the same time.

Add a dash of Brandy.

Dress with fruit and serve with Straws.

61. CHAMPAGNE SOUR

Fill medium Bar glass 1/3 full Shaved Ice.

3 dashes Lemon Juice.
Fill up with Champagne.
Add a dash of Brandy.
Stir gently, dress with Fruit and Berries; and serve with Straws.

62. CHAMPAGNE VELVET

Fill Goblet ½ full ice-cold Champagne.
Fill up balance of Goblet with ice-cold Porter.
Stir and serve.

PORTER – an extra dark strong ale similar to a Stout. In fact, it is difficult for the average consumer to distinguish between a Porter and a Stout, as the differences can be greater between brewers than between the types brewed. Generally, Porters will be sweeter with more pale ale malt and less roasted barley. Early Stouts were labeled "Extra" or "Double" or "Stout" Porters because of the slighter differences, but eventually just became known simply as "Stout". Today a sweeter Stout may be substituted for a Porter.

63. CLARET AND ICE

4 lumps Ice in medium size Mineral Water glass.

Fill up with Claret and serve.

◇◇

A Mineral Water Glass has a short stem, full cup and wide mouth. It is similar to a Beer glass, but shorter with a broader base.

◇◇

64. CLARET COBBLER

Dissolve one teaspoonful of Sugar with little Water in large Bar glass.

1 quartered slice Orange.

2 jiggers Claret.

Fill up with Shaved Ice and serve with Straws.

◇◇

CLARET is the British name for the blended red wine from the Bordeaux region in France. It was traditionally made with Cabernet Sauvignon, Cabernet Franc, Merlot, Petit Verdot, Malbec and sometimes Carménère. The term "Claret" may derive from the Latin "clarita"s which means "clarity" or "brilliance" as it is typically a light red. The region of Bordeaux was controlled by England for about 300 years beginning in the 12th century, hence it adopting a British name. Claret is actually a protected name in the European Union. In America it's known as Meritage. May substitute with light/dry red table wine.

◇◇

65. CLARET PUNCH

Fill large Bar glass 2/3 full Shaved Ice.

3 teaspoonfuls Bar Sugar.

4 dashes Lemon Juice.

2 slices Orange.

2 jiggers Claret.

Shake; strain into thin glass; dress with Fruit and serve with Straws.

66. CLUB COCKTAIL

Fill large Bar glass ½ full Shaved Ice.

2 dashes Angostura Bitters.

2 dashes Pineapple Syrup.

1 jigger Brandy.

Add a dash of Champagne.

Stir and strain into Cocktail glass.

Serve dressed with Berries and a twisted slice of Lemon Skin.

67. CLUB HOUSE CLARET PUNCH

Fill large Bar glass ¾ full Shaved Ice.

4 dashes Gum Syrup.

1 teaspoonful Lemon Juice.

1 teaspoonful Orange Juice.

2 jiggers Claret.

Shake; strain into tall, thin glass; fill up with Apollinaris or Seltzer. Dress with Fruit and serve.

68. COHASSET PUNCH

Fill large Bar glass ½ full Shaved Ice.

1 jigger New England Rum.

1 jigger Vermouth.

3 dashes Gum Syrup.

1 dash Orange Bitters.

½ juice of a Lemon

Stir and serve with a Preserved Peach and its liquor.

NEW ENGLAND RUM was produced during colonial times and continued up until Prohibition, when the already struggling distilleries were unable to continue production. It was also known as Medford rum for the Massachusetts town of Medford where most of the rum distilleries were located. The rum was dark and of high proof similar to the "Navy" or "London Dock" rums produced along the Thames River in England. Lamb's Navy Rum is a variety of navy rum still available, but may be hard to find in the States. May substitute with other dock or dark rums.

69. COLUMBIA SKIN
(also known as Whiskey Skin)

In a small bar glass add:

1 wine-glass Scotch whisky

1 piece lemon peel

½ tumbler water boiling

Serve.

70. CONTINENTAL SOUR

Fill a large Bar glass 2/3 full Shaved Ice.

1 teaspoonful Bar Sugar dissolved in little Water.

Juice of ½ Lemon.

1 jigger of either Whiskey, Brandy or Gin, as preferred.
Add a dash of Claret.

Shake; strain into Sour glass and serve.

71. COOPERSTOWN COCKTAIL

Use a large Bar glass. Fill with Lump Ice.

One jigger of Sir Robert Burnette's Old Tom Gin.
½ pony of Italian Vermouth.
Six leaves of fresh Mint.

Shake ingredients well together. Strain and serve in Cocktail glass.

72. CORDIAL LEMONADE

Add to a plain Lemonade 1/3 Jigger of any Cordial which the customer may prefer, and serve. Examples of popular Cordials you may want to try are: Amaretto (almond), Chambord (raspberry), Cointreau (orange), Drambuie (honey), Grand Marnier (orange), Sambuca (black licorice), and Southern Comfort (peaches).

73. COUPEREE
A soda float with a kick!

Fill large Bar glass 1/3 full Ice Cream.

¾ jigger Brandy.

1 pony Curacoa.

Mix thoroughly with a spoon.

Fill up with Plain Soda; grate Nutmeg on top and serve.

A soda float with a kick!

74. CREME DE MENTHE

Fill a Sherry glass with Shaved Ice.

1 pony Creme de Menthe.

Cut Straw in two pieces and serve.

CRÈME DE MENTHE is a spearmint or peppermint flavored liqueur with a neutral spirit base. It is available as both clear and green-colored and is widely available. Its name is French for "mint cream" though there is no cream in the recipe. It is also enjoyed as a digestif after meals as mint is known to help the digestive process. Many recipes also call for Crème de Menthe in cooking as a flavoring. You can make your own pretty simply in about 2 days with sugar, 80 proof vodka and fresh mint leaves. Substitution should not be necessary, but in a pinch use peppermint schnapps.

75. CURACOA

Into a bottle which will hold at least a quart, drop 6 ounces of Orange Peel sliced very thin, and add 1 pint of Whiskey. Cork the bottle securely and let it stand two weeks, shaking the bottle frequently during that time. Next, strain the mixture and add Syrup (2 cups sugar dissolved in 1 ½ cups water). Pour the strained mixture back into a clean bottle and let it stand 3 days, shaking well now and then during the first day. Optional - pour a teacupful of the mixture into a mortar and beat up with it 1 drachm Powdered Alum, 1 drachm Carbonate of Potash. Put this mixture back into the bottle and let it stand for 10 days, at the expiration of which time the Curacoa will be clear and ready for use.

CARBONATE OF POTASH is also known as Potassium carbonate. POWDERED ALUM is available in the spice section of the grocery store and was once used in pickling. Alum has been implicated in health problems, so many have discontinued its use. This recipe only calls for Potassium carbonate and Alum in order to clear the otherwise opaque liqueur. The flavor will not be diminished if you choose to use your homemade liqueur without using these additives to clear the liquid.

76. CURACOA PUNCH

Fill large Bar glass ¾ full Shaved Ice.

2 teaspoonfuls Bar Sugar.

4 dashes Lemon Juice.

1 pony Red Curacoa.

1 jigger Brandy.

½ pony Jamaica Rum.

Stir; decorate with Fruit and Serve with Straws.

77. CURRANT SHRUB

In a vessel which can be heated over a fire, mix:

1½ lbs. Cut Loaf Sugar.

1 quart Currant Juice

Place vessel on the fire and let it boil slowly for 10 minutes, and skim well while boiling. Then remove vessel from fire and add ½ gill of Brandy to every pint of Shrub. Bottle and cork securely. This drink is served by simply pouring a little of the Syrup into Ice Water, as any drink from Fruit Syrup is prepared. The basis preparation for all Shrubs or Small Fruits, such as Cherries, Raspberries, etc., is prepared in the same way as directed for Currant Shrub, varying the quantity of Sugar used to suit the kind of Fruit.

◇◇

CURRANT JUICE is derived from the Black Currant berry, which, funny enough was banned in the U.S. for almost 100 years. It was considered a "forbidden fruit" because it was erroneously blamed for a disease in white pines. It wasn't until the 1960's that the Federal government turned jurisdiction of the ban over to the states. In 2003, New York finally overturned the ban. Several states still have the ban on their books. Black currents have just recently been making a comeback. They are highly nutritious, having the most antioxidants in a juice test, among many other benefits. Black currents are quite sour and require additional sweetening. A few juice makers now have Black Current juice among their offerings. Check your local grocery for availability.

◇◇

78. DELUSION

Use a large Mixing glass; fill with Shaved Ice.

½ Lime Juice.
2/3 white Creme de Menthe.
1/3 Apricot Brandy.

Shake well; strain into thin Stem glass and serve.

79. DERONDA COCKTAIL

Fill large Bar glass with Shaved Ice.

1½ jiggers Calisaya.

1½ jiggers Plymouth Gin.

Shake; strain into Cocktail glass and serve.

This recipes call for two, and only two, ingredients that appear in no other recipe in this collection. Both ingredients have some fascinating history which follows:

◇◇◇◇◇◇◇◇◇◇◇◇◇◇◇◇◇◇◇◇◇◇◇◇◇◇◇◇◇◇◇◇◇◇◇

CALISAYA is an aromatic herbal bitters made primarily by infusing the bark of the Cinchona plant in a neutral grain spirit. Other barks, roots, herbs, spices and flowers may also be used. The Cinchona plant is native to Peru, Bolivian and Ecuador. It is known as the "fever tree" for the quinine it produces, which is a treatment for Malaria and a muscle relaxant which helps to relieve shivering. Because of Prohibition, the calisaya liqueur had completely disappeared from the US market until the Oregan based Elixir, Inc. reconstructed the bitters under the trademarked the name Calisaya. More information is available on their website - http://www.elixir-us.com.

◇◇◇◇◇◇◇◇◇◇◇◇◇◇◇◇◇◇◇◇◇◇◇◇◇◇◇◇◇◇◇◇◇◇◇

◇◇◇◇◇◇◇◇◇◇◇◇◇◇◇◇◇◇◇◇◇◇◇◇◇◇◇◇◇◇◇◇◇◇◇

PLYMOUTH GIN is a gin so called because it is distilled in Plymouth, England (not Massachusetts). There is only one remaining brand in production, that of the Black Friars Distillery, which has been in operation since 1793. It was founded as Fox & Williamson, then soon became Coates & Co., which it remained until March 2004 when it was renamed to Black Friars Distillery. The current name was probably inspired by the distillery being in a former monastery dating back to 1431.

◇◇◇◇◇◇◇◇◇◇◇◇◇◇◇◇◇◇◇◇◇◇◇◇◇◇◇◇◇◇◇◇◇◇◇

80. DIARRHEA DRAUGHT

Into a Whiskey glass pour:

½ jigger Blackberry Brandy.

½ pony Peach Brandy.

2 dashes Jamaica Ginger.

Grate Nutmeg on top and serve.

◇◇◇◇◇◇◇◇◇◇◇◇◇◇◇◇◇◇◇◇◇◇◇◇◇◇◇◇◇◇◇◇◇◇◇

This cocktail would have been ordered by a customer to treat an upset stomach. Its several ingredients combine to treat a variety of intestinal discomforts. The Brandy is thought to warm and settle the stomach. The ginger would serve to reduce nausea and reflux. The Blackberry is the real hero here. Its high concentration of tannins is believed to help tighten the mucous membranes of the intestinal tract, reducing watery stools. Urban legend is that traveling salesmen carried a flask of blackberry brandy in case of an unfamiliar meal upsetting the stomach. Don't rely on this to replace all the lost fluids, but it should help to heal what ails you.

◇◇◇◇◇◇◇◇◇◇◇◇◇◇◇◇◇◇◇◇◇◇◇◇◇◇◇◇◇◇◇◇◇◇◇

81. DIXIE COCKTAIL

Add to a plain Whiskey Cocktail:

1 dash Curacoa.
6 drops Creme de Menthe.

82. DORAY SOUR

Fill large Bar glass 2/3 full Shaved Ice.

3 dashes Gum Syrup
4 dashes Lemon Juice.
1 dash Lime Juice.
1 teaspoonful Abricontine or green Chartreuse.
½ jigger Tokay or Sweet Catawba Wine.
½ jigger Brandy.

Stir well and strain into a fancy Sour glass; dress with Fruits; dash with Apollinaris or Seltzer; top off with a little Claret and serve.

83. DUPLEX COCKTAIL

Fill large Bar glass with Shaved Ice.

1/3 Jigger Old Tom Gin.
1 pony Italian Vermouth.
1 pony French Vermouth.
3 dashes Acid Phosphate.
4 dashes Orange Bitters.

Shake; strain into Cocktail glass and serve.

ACID PHOSPHATE is a liquid suspension of Phosphoric Acid, Calcium Phosphate, Magnesium Phosphate, Potassium Phosphate in water. Considered a health tonic in its day, it adds a touch of "tartness" or "dryness" to cocktails. It was also used as a substitute for lemon or lime juice. It may be substituted with lemon juice, though that will add flavor that the acid phosphate would not. Never use phosphoric acid! The phosphoric acid in this mixture is buffered so that it is not harmful. Straight phosphoric acid will cause injury. You will probably have to special order Acid Phosphate, though a bottle will last a long time. It may appear cloudy, but not to worry, any undissolved salts do not affect the taste of the product.

84. DURKEE COCKTAIL

Fill large Bar glass 2/3 Full Shaved Ice.

1 tablespoonful Bar Sugar.

4 dashes Lemon Juice.

3 dashes Curacoa.

1 jigger Jamaica Rum.

Shake well; strain into tall, thin glass; fill up with Plain Soda; stir gently and serve.

85. EAGLE PUNCH

Into a Hot Water glass drop:

1 lump Cut Loaf Sugar and dissolve in little Hot Water, crushing with a muddler.

½ jigger Bourbon Whiskey.

½ jigger Rye Whiskey.

Fill up with boiling Water; twist a piece of Lemon Peel and grate Nutmeg on top and serve.

86. EAST INDIA COCKTAIL

Fill large Bar glass ¾ full Shaved Ice.

3 dashes Maraschino.

3 dashes Red Curacoa.

3 dashes Angostura Bitters.

1 jigger Brandy.

Stir well; strain into Cocktail glass and serve with a piece of twisted Lemon Peel on top.

87. EL DORADO PUNCH

Fill large Bar glass nearly full Shaved Ice.

1 tablespoonful Bar Sugar.

¼ jigger Whiskey.

¼ jigger Jamaica Rum.

½ jigger Brandy.

1 slice Lemon.

Shake; dress with Fruit and serve with Straws.

88. ENGLISH BISHOP PUNCH

Roast an Orange before a fire or in a hot oven. When brown, cut it in quarters and drop the pieces, with a few Cloves, into a small stove pot, and pour in 1 quart of hot Port Wine. Add 6 lumps Cut Loaf Sugar and let the mixture simmer over heat for 30 minutes. Serve in Stem glasses with Nutmeg grated on top.

89. FANCY WHISKEY SMASH

Fill large Bar glass ½ full Shaved Ice.

2 teaspoonfuls Bar Sugar.

3 sprigs Mint pressed with muddler in 1 jigger aerated Water.

1 jigger Whiskey.

Stir well; strain into Sour glass; dress with Fruit and serve.

◇◇

Why is MINT so popular in cocktails? The cool, refreshing and slightly sweet herb enhances the scrumptious flavors of fruit and complements the intensity of alcohol. Mint is incredibly easy to grow in containers, or in an herb garden, and is widely available. You can grow peppermint or spearmint or both. They are both from the genus Mentha but do have some important differences. Spearmint's scientific name is "Mentha spicata" and has the chemical "carvone" which gives it that sweet flavor. Spearmint is used more often in cooking. Peppermint's scientific name is "Mentha piperita" and is considered more medicinal. Peppermint has a high menthol content (40% compared to just 0.05% in spearmint). Menthol is responsible for that cool sensation, when we taste it or feel it on our skin, by activating sensory receptors that tell us there is something cold. However there is no actual temperature change in our mouth or skin. Add 6 to 8 mint leaves when cocktails call for mint.

◇◇

90. FEDORA

Fill large Bar glass ¾ full Shaved Ice.

2 teaspoonfuls Bar Sugar dissolved in little Water.

1 pony Curacoa.

1 pony Brandy.

½ pony Jamaica Rum.

½ pony Whiskey.

Shake well; dress with Fruit and serve with Straws.

91. FOG HORN
Country Club Style

Use a large Mixing glass; fill with Lump Ice.

½ Lime Juice.

½ Lemon Juice.

1 teaspoonful Bar Sugar.

1 jigger Burnette's Old Tom Gin.

Stir well; strain into tall, thin glass and fill with imported Ginger Ale.

◊◊◊

LEMONS and LIMES, what's the difference? There are important differences between the two, so when a recipe calls for a Lemon, don't use a Lime and vice versa. Sometimes recipes call for both, like the above Fog Horn, so you'll really do need both. Here's why: Lemons are larger than limes and have more juice, so juice from half a lemon will be more than juice from half a lime. Lemons are more bitter/sour and limes are more tart with slightly higher acidity. They obviously have a color difference which will impact your beverage as well. Suffice to say; when you substitute one for another, you have a whole new drink. Examples of cocktails where this is the only difference are the Lemon Drop (vodka with lemon juice) and the Gimlet (vodka with lime juice).

◊◊◊

92. FRENCH POUSSE CAFE

Fill a Pousse Cafe glass ½ full of Maraschino and add: Raspberry Syrup, Vanilla, Curacoa, Chartreuse and Brandy in equal proportions until the glass is filled. The ingredients should be poured in one after the other with great care, to prevent the colors from blending. Ignite the Brandy on top, and after it has blazed for a few seconds extinguishing it by placing a saucer or the bottom of another glass over the blazing fluid. Then serve.

93. GIBSON COCKTAIL

Use a large Mixing glass with Lump Ice.

1 jigger Gordon Gin.

1 pony French Vermouth.

Stir; strain and serve in Cocktail glass.

Gordon's Gin is a proprietary London dry gin known for being named in Ian Fleming's 1953 novel Casino Royale. The gin dates back to 1769 with a closely held recipe since that time, known by only twelve people in the world. What is known is that the gin is triple-distilled, derived from wheat grains and contains flavors of juniper berries, coriander seeds, angelica root, liquorice, orris root, orange and lemon peel. It does not add sugar, which makes it a "dry" gin. James Bond's Vesper Cocktail in Casino Royale is given the famous mixing instruction of "shaken, not stirred". This method dilutes the high alcohol content of Gordon's gin with the ice.

94. GILLETTE COCKTAIL
Chicago Style

Use a large Mixing glass; fill with Lump Ice.

Juice ½ Lime.
1½ jiggers Burnette's Old Tom Gin.
½ teaspoonful Bar Sugar.

Stir well and strain into Cocktail glass.

95. GIN AND CALAMUS
(for historic purposes only – use a substitute for Calamus)

Steep a substitute for "Calamus Root" in water.

Put ½ oz. of substitute "Calamus Root" water into a quart bottle of Gin.

Serve as you would a Straight Drink.

◇◇◇

WARNING – The FDA has banned any use of Calamus in food products because they claim it contains Beta-asarone, a carcinogen (toxic) which in high doses causes hallucinations. The amount of Beta-asarone varies wildly between plants so, without testing, it is unknown if it is safe to use internally. Extracts of Calamus are available for external use but are not intended for consumption. Recommended substitutes for Calamus include ginger, cinnamon and nutmeg.

◇◇◇

◇◇◇

Calamus Root is an ancient aromatic reed native to Asia which grows in marshy conditions. It is mentioned 5 times in the Bible (Exodus 30:23, Song of Solomon 4:14, Ezekiel 27:19, Isaiah 43:24 and Jeremiah 6:20) and was an ingredient in the anointing oil for the Tabernacle. Calamus is also known as Sweet Sledge, Sweet Myrtle and Sweet Flag. Traditionally, Calamus was used for its benefits to the digestive system and the lungs. It was thought to eliminate phlegm, clear congestion, and treat chronic bronchitis and bronchial asthma. It helped to reduce acidity and ease heartburn. It was also used to calm the mind and treat insomnia. Traditional Chinese medicine touts Calamus for treating deafness, dizziness and epilepsy in addition to vomiting, diarrhea, abdominal pain, and dysentery. In Ayurvedic Medicine, Calamus is used to promote circulation to the brain, sharpening memory, and enhancing awareness. The root's oil produces a strong and fragrant aroma. Its active elements are released by boiling in water, turning it pale yellow. Calamus is still used externally in baths or as a rub for sore muscles and to improve circulation.

◇◇◇

Song of Solomon 4:13-16

Your shoots are an orchard of pomegranates with
choice fruits, henna with nard plants,
Nard and saffron, calamus and cinnamon, with all the trees
of frankincense, myrrh and aloes, along with all the finest spices.
You are a garden spring, a well of fresh water,
and streams flowing from Lebanon.
Awake, O north wind, And come, wind of the south; Make my
garden breathe out fragrance, Let its spices be wafted abroad.
May my beloved come into his garden And eat its choice fruits!

96. GIN DAISY

Juice of ½ of a Lime.

1 pony Cusenier Grenadine.

1 jigger Sir Robert Burnette's Old Tom Gin.

Serve in a Mug with Lump Ice; fill with Seltzer.

Stir well and decorate with the skin of the Lime and fresh Mint and serve with Straws.

97. GIN SOUR
Country Club Style

Use a large Mixing glass.

Fill with Lump Ice.

½ Lime Juice.

½ Orange Juice.

2 dashes Pineapple Juice.

½ pony Rock Candy Syrup.

1 jigger Burnette's Old Tom Gin.

Shake well; strain into Cocktail glass and serve.

◇◇

ROCK CANDY SYRUP is sweeter and thicker than simple syrup. It can be made easily at home by bringing 2 parts sugar and 1 part water to a boil, then lowering to a simmer for 5 minutes. Remove from heat and cool before using.

◇◇

98. GIN SQUASH
Country Club Style

Use a large glass Stein; fill with Lump Ice.

1 pony Lemon Juice.

1 jigger Orange Juice.

1 pony Pineapple Juice.

1 pony Rock Candy Syrup.

1 jigger Burnette's Old Tom Gin.

Fill with Seltzer: stir well and serve.

99. HORSE THIEF COCKTAIL

Fill a large Mixing glass with Lump Ice.

2 dashes green Absinthe.

½ pony Italian Vermouth.

1 jigger Sir Robert Burnette's Old Tom Gin.

Stir well and serve in a Cocktail glass.

100. IRISH ROSE
Country Club Style

Use a tall, thin glass; fill with Cracked Ice.

1 pony imported Grenadine.

1 jigger Old Bushmill Whiskey.

Fill with Seltzer.

Stir well and serve.

OLD BUSHMILL WHISKEY *is from the Old Bushmills Distillery in Northern Ireland. The whiskey dates back to 1608 when the original land owner received a license to distill whiskey. The distillery itself dates back to 1784 though was occasionally closed in the 1800's. After a 1885 fire, it was rebuilt and has been in continuous operation ever since. The Old Bushmills Distillery is a popular tourist attraction. It boasts using the "sweetest and smoothest water in Ireland" from the River Bush tributary, Saint Columb's Rill, to produce the spirits. Old Bushmills offerings have received acclaim at international Spirit competitions with its Black Bush Finest Blended Whiskey receiving double gold medals in the San Francisco World Spirits Competitions of 2007 and 2010. At the 2008 and 2011 Beverage Testing Institute ratings, it received a well-above-average score of 93. If unable to obtain, substitute with Irish whiskey.*

101. JERSEY LIGHTNING COCKTAIL

Use large Mixing glass; fill with Lump Ice.

1 jigger Apple Jack Brandy.
1 pony Italian Vermouth.

Stir well; strain and serve in Cocktail glass.

102. KNABENSCHUE
Country Club Style

Use a small stone Mug; Lump Ice.

1 lump Sugar.
2 dashes Angostura Bitters.

Fill with Champagne.

Stir well; dress with fresh Mint and serve.

◇◇

This cocktail is thought to be named after the famous aeronaut of the day, Roy KNABENSHUE, one of the first pilots in America to fly a steerable balloon. Knabenshue also piloted the first successful dirigible at the 1904 St. Louis World's Fair and built the first passenger dirigible, named White City, in America in 1913. The picture below shows the famous airship "California Arrow" which Knabenshue flew at the World's Fair in St. Louis.

◇◇

103. L.P.W.

Use a large Mixing glass.

Fill with Lump See.
1 jigger of Sir Robert Burnette's Old Tom Gin.

½ pony of Italian Vermouth.

½ pony of French Vermouth.

Stir well and strain into a Cocktail glass. Add a Pickeled coctail Onion and serve.

104. LEAPING FROG

1 jigger Hungarian Apricot Brandy.

Juice of ½ Lime.

Fill glass with Lump Ice.

Shake well and strain into Stem glass.

◇◇

HUNGARIAN APRICOT BRANDY is known today as Barack Palinka. It is an un-aged, unsweetened, apricot Brandy produced and sold in Hungary and Eastern Europe. It may be available through online ordering or you can substitute with any "eau de vie" – un-aged, unsweetened fruit Brandy.

◇◇

105. LONE TREE COCKTAIL

Use a large Mixing glass; fill with Lump Ice.

1 jigger Burnette's Old Tom Gin.

1/3 Italian Vermouth.

1/3 French Vermouth.

Shake well; serve in Cocktail glass.

106. MINT JULEP
Kentucky Style

Use a large Silver Mug.

Dissolve one lump of Sugar in one-half pony of Water.

Fill mug with Fine Ice.

Two jiggers of Old Bourbon Whiskey.

Stir well; add one sprig of Mint and serve. Be careful and not bruise the Mint.

◇◇

The modern recipe for Mint Julep pictured below is essentially the same. The only difference is the use of powdered sugar, which would dissolve more easily with stirring than a lump of sugar.

◇◇

107. OJEN COCKTAIL

Use an old-fashion Toddy glass.

1 lump Ice.

Juice of ½ of a Lime.

1 dash Angostura Bitters.

2 dashes of Seltzer Water.

Stir well and serve.

108. OLD FASHION COCKTAIL

Use a Toddy glass.

1 lump of Ice.

2 dashes of Angostura Bitters.

1 lump of Sugar and dissolve in Water.

1½ jiggers of Bourbon Whiskey.

Twist piece of Lemon Skin over the drink and drop it in. Stir well and serve.

The modern Old Fashioned recipe pictured here is identical except for the terminology, showing a great recipe stands the test of time.

109. ONION COCKTAIL

Fill large Bar glass with Cracked Ice.

1 jigger of Burnette's Tom Gin.
½ pony of Italian Vermouth and no Bitters used.

Stir well. Strain and serve with a cocktail Onion.

110. OVERALL JULEP
St. Louis Style

Use a large Mixing glass; fill with Lump Ice.

2/3 Wineglass Rye Whiskey.
2/3 Wineglass Gordon Gin.
½ Wineglass Imported Grenadine.

Juice ½ Lemon.

Juice ½ Lime.

Shake well; pour into tall, thin glass; add one bottle Imported Club Soda and serve.

111. PEQUOT SEMER

Use a tall, thin Bar glass.

Juice of a Lime.

Three sprigs of fresh Mint.

1 dash Cusenier Grenadine.

½ pony Pineapple Juice.

½ pony Orange Juice.

1 jigger of Sir Robert Burnette's Old Tom Gin.

Crush ingredients together; fill with Lump Ice; add Seltzer. Stir well and serve.

112. POLO PLAYERS' DELIGHT
Horse's Neck

Use a tall, thin glass.

1 lump Ice.

1 jigger Sir Robert Burnette's Old Tom Gin.

1 Cantrell & Cochran's Ginger Ale.

Stir well and serve.

Cantrell & Cochran's Ginger Ale was a brand name ginger ale im-

ported from Belfast, Northern Ireland. The soft drink business was founded by Dr. Thomas Cantrell in 1852, and Alderman Henry Cochrane became his partner in 1868, establishing Cantrell & Cochrane. The company made ginger ale, seltzer water, and medicated aerated water in round-bottom bottles. This was a signature element to keep the corks from drying out, because the bottle had to be laid on its side. The company is still in business today with locations all over Northern Ireland. Cantrell & Cochrane is now known as C&C Group. Ginger Ale is available through their Finches Soft Drinks line sold under the C&C Gleeson division.

113. POUSSE CAFE
St. Louis

Pour in Pousse Cafe glass as follows:

1/6 glass Raspberry Syrup.

1/6 glass Maraschino.

1/6 glass Green Vanilla.

1/6 glass Curacao.

1/6 glass Yellow Chartreuse.

1/6 glass Brandy.

In preparing the above use a small Wineglass with spoon for pouring in each Cordial separately. Be careful they do not mix together.

GREEN VANILLA CORDIAL was made by macerating vanilla bean pods in water and a neutral alcohol, such as vodka, for several days. The extract was then distilled. Sugar was added to the distillate, as well as color, if desired. Until the mid 1800's vanilla was only grown in Mexico, so this is an example of a flavor that was brought to the old world from the new. Early efforts to grow the orchid vine else-

where failed because the plant has a very short and finicky pollination period. In Mexico, the abeja de monte, or mountain bee, knew just when and how to enter and pollinate each flower. The flowers would then become vanilla bean pods. It wasn't until the symbiotic relationship between the flowers and the bees was understood that the vanilla orchid was successfully pollinated by hand, bringing the vanilla orchid to other parts of the world. Today every vanilla bean outside of Mexico is still the result of hand pollination, which has to be done on the only day each flower blooms. With the right conditions it is possible to grow your own vanilla orchids and, with a small personal distillery, one could also make their own vanilla cordial. Or you could just substitute with a naturally flavored vanilla liqueur.

114. REMSEN COOLER

Use a medium size Fizz glass.

Peel a Lemon as you would an Apple.

Place the Rind or Peeling into the Fizz glass.

Add 2 or 3 lumps of Crystal Ice.

Historic Cocktails

1 Wineglass of Remsen Scotch Whiskey.

Fill up the balance with Club Soda; stir up slowly with a spoon and serve.

(Bartender's Note to Fellow Bartenders: In this country it is often the ease that people call a Remsen Cooler where they want Old Tom Gin or Sloe Gin instead of Scotch Whiskey. It is therefore the bartender's duty to mix as desired.)

◇◇◇

There never was such a thing as REMSEN SCOTCH WHISKEY so why does this recipe call for it? It seems that as these classic recipes were passed around the country clubs and city clubs, the names of those who invented the drink could get confused with the ingredients in the drink. In this case the whiskey actually called for was Ramsay's Scotch Whiskey from the Port Ellen distillery owned by John Ramsay on the Scottish island of Islay. John Ramsay was one of the first people to export Scotch to America, thus the whiskey being known by his name. The recipe, however, was named for William R. Remsen, a member of New York's exclusive Union club. The similarity of the names Remsen and Ramsay must have led to the mislabeling of the whiskey in the recipe. Substitute with your Scotch whiskey of choice.

◇◇◇

115. SEPTEMBER MORN COCKTAIL
Country Club Style

Use a large Mixing glass; fill with Lump Ice.

½ Lime Juice.
1 jigger Burnette's Old Tom Gin.
2 dashes Imported Grenadine.

Shake well; strain into Cocktail glass and serve.

116. SHANDY GAFF

Use a large Bar glass.
Fill half the glass with Porter and half with Ginger Ale.
It can also be made with half Ale and half Ginger Ale.

117. SHERRY AND BITTERS

Put 2 dashes Dr. Siegert's genuine Angostura Bitters in a Sherry glass.
Roll the glass 'till the Bitters entirely cover the inside surface.
Fill the glass with Sherry and serve.

The modern, modest SHERRY is one of the world's oldest wines. It is thought to date back 1000 years before the Common Era (1000 BCE or 1000 BC). It originated with the early Phoenician settlements in the Iberian Peninsula, today Spain and Portugal. Over the centuries the region and the wine were influenced by the Greeks, Romans, Moors, Spanish and British. Sherry is a white wine fortified typically with Brandy after fermentation. Sherry is also known as "sack" from the Spanish word "saca" meaning extraction. Sherry is a protected designation in Europe, where under Spanish law, all wine labeled "Sherry" must come from the Sherry Triangle in the province of Cádiz. Many wine critics consider Sherry an under-appreciated and neglected wine. So give Sherry a try, and see if it deserves a rebirth of admiration.

118. STINGER
Country Club Style

Use a large Mixing glass; fill with Lump Ice.

1 jigger Old Brandy.

1 pony white Creme de Menthe.

Shake well; strain into Cocktail glass and serve.

The modern Stinger recipe shown uses metric measurements, so the amount of Cognac (instead of Brandy) is slightly more than 1 jigger, and the amount of Crème de Menthe is slightly less than 1 pony.

119. STONE SOUR

Use a tall, thin glass; fill with fine Ice.

½ pony Lemon Juice.
½ pony Orange Juice.
2 dashes Rock Candy Syrup.
1 jigger Old Tom Gin.

Leave in Ice; stir well and serve.

120. TOM TOM

Use a large Brandy Roller glass.

Fill Roller half full of Fine Ice.

Add 1 pony of Old Brandy.

Add 1 jigger of green Creme de Menthe

Serve.

121. TWILIGHT COCKTAIL

Use a large Mixing glass with Lump Ice.

1 jigger Bourbon.

½ pony Italian Vermouth.

Juice of whole Lime.

Shake well; strain into a Champagne glass; fill with Seltzer and serve.

122. WHISKEY
Scotch Hot

1 lump Sugar dissolved in Hot Whiskey glass.

1 jigger Scotch Whiskey.
Fill up with Hot Water.
1 slice Lemon Peel.

Stir and serve with Nutmeg sprinkled on top.

123. WHISKEY
Irish Hot

1 lump Sugar dissolved in Hot Whiskey glass.

1 jigger Irish Whiskey.
Fill up with Hot Water.
1 slice Lemon Peel.

Stir and serve with Nutmeg sprinkled on top.

124. WHISKEY PUNCH
St. Louis Style

Use a large Mixing glass; fill with Lump Ice.

One jigger Bourbon Whiskey.

½ pony Italian Vermouth.

½ pony Pineapple Syrup.

½ pony Lemon Juice.

Shake well; strain into Stem glass and serve.

Cocktail Recipes with Egg

Raw egg in many beverages is an added ingredient for its nutritional value, but its use in cocktails goes beyond nourishment. The egg imparts "foaminess" to the beverage and acts as an emulsifying (evenly dispersing) agent. In some recipes the egg is served whole and the recipient is free to mix it in if they wish. When yolk and white are served separate you may see the term "golden" for the use of the egg yolk or "silver" for the use of the egg white. Egg whites are more often called for than yolks as they provide an unparalleled froth to beverages.

1. ALE FLIP

Fill an Ale glass nearly full.

Add 1 teaspoonful of Bar Sugar.

Break in 1 whole Egg; grate a little Nutmeg on top and serve the drink with a spoon alongside of the glass.

2. BISMARCK

In Sherry Wine glass gently add:

2 teaspoonfuls Vanilla Cordial in Sherry Wine glass.

1 yolk of an Egg covered with Benedictine so as not to break the yolk.

½ wineglass Kuemmel.

1 light dash Angostura Bitters.

The colors should be kept separate and great care exercised to prevent the ingredients from running together.

◇◇

KUEMMEL (Kümmel) is a caraway liqueur made from crushed caraway seed, crushed fennel seed, ground cumin, grain alcohol and sugar. Originated in Northern Europe and is now made in Scandinavia.

◇◇

3. BRACE UP

In large Mixing glass add:

1 tablespoonful Bar Sugar

3 dashes Boker's or Angostura Bitters.

3 dashes Lemon Juice.

2 dashes Anisette.

1 Egg.

1 jigger Brandy

½ glass Shaved Ice.

Shake well; strain into tall, thin glass; fill with Apollinaris and serve.

◇◇

Boker's Bitters was one of the many near fatalities of The Volstead Act, known as Prohibition, causing the company to close down in the 1920's. The Boker"s company was founded by John G. Boker in 1828 and their bitters were widely acclaimed around the world for refined drinks during cocktails' pre-prohibition Golden Age. A re-formulated version was released in August 2009 under the name "Dr. Adam Elmegirab's Boker's Cocktail Bitters". It is crafted with spirits, water, herbs, spices, caramel and seven botanicals including orange peel, quassia bark, catechu, cardamom and mallow flowers.

◇◇

4. BRANDY FLIP

Fill medium. Bar glass ¼ full Shaved Ice.

1 Egg broken in whole.

2 level teaspoonfuls Bar Sugar.

1 jigger Brandy.

Shake well; strain into small Shell glass; grate a little Nutmeg on top and serve.

◇◇◇

Nutmeg is the seed of a tree indigenous to the Spice Islands of Indonesia. It has a strong, citrusy sour flavor – a little goes a long way. Keep a nutmeg seed at your bar and grate just a touch of it onto your cocktail creations to add another dimension of flavor. Besides its cocktail enhancing qualities, nutmeg can improve your health. The benefits of nutmeg include lower blood pressure, less bad breath, a better night's sleep, stronger bones, improved digestion, elimination of kidney stones and toxins, fighting cancer growth, improving brain function, reducing skin irritation and lessening pain associated with wounds, injuries or arthritis.

◇◇◇

5. CHOCOLATE PUNCH

Fill large Bar glass 2/3 full Shaved Ice.

1 teaspoonful Bar Sugar.

¼ jigger Curacoa.

1 jigger Port Wine.

1 Egg.

Fill up with Milk.

Shake well; strain into Punch glass; grate Nutmeg on top and serve.

◇◇

For all recipes which call for milk, this author recommends Raw Milk. Why? Raw Milk is loaded with healthy bacteria (i.e.Lactobacilli) which are good for your gut, is high in omega-3 and low omega-6, has more than 60 digestive enzymes (which are killed by pasteurization leading to problems with milk digestion), has beneficial growth factors and antibodies, and is chalked full of vitamins A, B, C, D, E, and K as well as calcium, magnesium, phosphorus, and iron in highly bioavailable forms. Raw Milk is also rich in conjugated linoleic acid (CLA), healthy unoxidized cholesterol, beneficial raw fats, amino acids, and proteins, all in highly bioavailable forms and 100% percent digestible. The phosphatase in Raw Milk helps the absorption of calcium by your bones, and its lipase enzyme helps to hydrolyze and absorb fats. The process of pasteurization, however, pretty much reverses all of those benefits, turns the naturally healthy fat into an unhealthy fat, and the resulting dead milk actually promotes pathogens. To set the record straight on Raw Milk, there were only 1,100 illnesses caused by Raw Milk between 1973 and 2009 and zero deaths. However in the same time period, there were 422,000 illnesses and at least 50 deaths caused by pasteurized milk or cheese. Raw Milk has been enjoyed by humanity, without civilization coming to an end, for thousands of years. It is only in very recent human history that we have killed the beverage with pasteurization. As the owner of two Jersey milk cows I admit total bias on this topic, but I encourage you to look more into this issue on your own. The government has done a good job of demonizing us Raw Milk producers, kind of like they demonized alcohol to get the 18th Amendment ratified. If you decide Raw Milk is for you, you don't have to own a milk cow to enjoy the delicate dairy the way God intended. There are several resources online to find sources of Raw Milk in your area such as www.realmilk.com/real-milk-finder.

6. CLARET FLIP

Fill large Bar glass ½ full Shaved Ice.

2 heaping teaspoonfuls Bar Sugar dissolved in a little Water.

1 whole Egg broken in.

1½ Jiggers Claret Wine.

Shake thoroughly; strain into Punch glass; sprinkle with Nutmeg on top and serve.

7. CLOVER CLUB COCKTAIL

Fill large Bar glass ½ full Fine Ice.

½ pony Raspberry Syrup.

½ jigger Dry Gin.

½ jigger French Vermouth.

White of 1 Egg.

Shake well; strain into Cocktail glass and serve.

This modern Clover Club recipe still calls for an egg white but leaves off the French Vermouth and instead adds Lemon Juice and more Gin.

8. CLOVER LEAF COCKTAIL

Fill Mixing glass with Lump Ice.

½ pony Grenadine.

The white of one Egg.

1 jigger Sir Robert Burnette's Old Tom Gin.

Shake well and strain into a Cocktail glass.

9. COFFEE COCKTAIL

Fill large Bar glass 2/3 full Shaved Ice.

1 fresh Egg.
1 teaspoonful Bar Sugar.
1 jigger Port Wine.
1 pony Brandy.

Shake; strain into medium thin glass; grate Nutmeg on top and serve.

10. COUNTRY COCKTAIL

Fill large Bar glass 2/3 full Shaved Ice.

1 teaspoonful Bar Sugar.
1 pony Brandy.
1 jigger Port Wine.
1 Egg.

Shake well; strain into thin glass; grate Nutmeg on top and serve.

11. DREAM

Fill large Bar glass 2/3 full Shaved Ice.

1 teaspoonful Bar Sugar.
3 dashes Lemon Juice.
1 white of an Egg.
1 Wineglass Milk and Cream.
1 jigger Tom Gin.

Shake thoroughly; strain into tall, thin glass; cover the top lightly with Creme de Menthe and serve.

12. DORAY PUNCH

Fill large Bar glass 2/3 full Shaved Ice.

2 teaspoonfuls Lemon Juice.
4 dashes Pineapple Syrup.
4 dashes Gum Syrup.
¼ jigger Jamaica Rum.
¼ jigger green Chartreuse.
½ jigger Tokay Wine.
½ jigger Brandy.
1 white of an Egg.

Shake hard; strain into thin Bar glass; dress with Fruit; dash with Seltzer; grate Nutmeg on top and serve.

13. EGG MILK PUNCH

Fill large Bar glass ½ full Shaved Ice.

2 teaspoonfuls Bar Sugar.

1 Egg

1 pony Santa Cruz Rum.

1 jigger Brandy.

Fill up with Milk; shake thoroughly until the mixture creams; strain into tall thin glass; grate Nutmeg on top and serve.

14. EGGNOG

Fill large Bar glass ½ full Shaved Ice.

1 Egg

1 teaspoonful Bar Sugar.

¾ jigger Brandy.

½ jigger Jamaica Rum.

Fill up with Milk; shake thoroughly; strain into tall, thin glass and serve with little Nutmeg grated on top.

15. FANNIE WARD

Use a large Mixing glass with Lump Ice.

White of an Egg.

Juice ½ Lime.

2 dashes imported Grenadine.

1 jigger Bacardi Rum.

Shake and strain into Cocktail glass.

16. FREE LOVE COCKTAIL
Club Style

Lump Ice. Use Shaker.

½ of the white of 1 Egg.

3 dashes Anisette.

1 jigger Old Tom Gin.

1 pony fresh Cream.

Shake well, serve in Cocktail glass.

17. RAMOS GIN FIZZ
Country Club Style

1 lump Ice.

1 dash Lemon Juice.

1 dash Orange Water.

White of Egg.

1 jigger Burnette's Old Tom Gin.

1 teaspoonful Powdered Sugar.

1 pony Milk.

1 dash Seltzer Water.

Shake well; strain into Highball glass and serve.

18. TOM AND JERRY

Make a batter by separating the yolks from whites of a given number of Eggs; beating the whites to a stiff froth and stirring the yolks until very thin. Then mix together in a Tom and Jerry bowl, stirring in Bar Sugar slowly until the batter is stiff. Use a ratio of 1 teaspoon sugar to 1 egg. Serve as follows:

Fill Tom and Jerry Mug ¼ full of Batter.

½ jigger Rum.

½ jigger Brandy.

Stir well with Bar spoon; fill up with Hot Water; stir more; grate Nutmeg on top and serve.

Non-Alcoholic Cocktail Recipes

1. APOLLINARIS LEMONADE

Fill large Bar glass 2/3 full Shaved Ice.

2 teaspoonfuls Powdered Sugar.

1 Lemon's Juice.

Fill up with Apollinaris or other sparkling mineral water.

Stir; strain into Lemonade glass dress with Fruit and serve.

2. AUDITORIUM COOLER

Into large Bar glass add:

Juice of 1 Lemon.

1 teaspoonful Bar Sugar.

1 bottle Ginger Ale off the ice.

Stir; decorate with Fruit and Berries, Serve.

3. BEEF TEA

½ teaspoonful Beef Extract in small Bar glass.

Fill glass with Hot Water. Stir well while seasoning with Pepper, Salt and Celery Salt. Serve with small glass of Cracked Ice and spoon on the side.

In the days before there were vitamins and minerals widely available, people had to make home remedies to heal what ailed them. Beef Tea is an example of a non-alcoholic cocktail that was thought to perk you up when you were worn out. Maybe it is due to the high dose of iron in beef extract? The concentrated nutrition? Theories abound, but until you try it, how will you know? Bovril dates back to the

1870's, when large quantities of beef were needed to feed Napoleon III's troops. Transporting that much beef was difficult, so a product called "Johnston's Fluid Beef" was developed. Later the product was renamed "Bovril". The "bo" referred to the Latin bovem for ox and the "vril", interestingly, referred to the fictional substance "vril" in the 1870 book "The Coming Race". The Vril-ya were a superior race of people empowered by "vril" so the makers of Bovril borrowed from the book's popularity in naming their product. Bovril is still available today and is the only all-natural beef extract found at the time of printing.

4. BLACK COW

Use a large Mixing glass with Lump Ice.

2 jiggers of Cream.

1 bottle Sarsaparilla soda.

Stir well and serve with Straws.

This is another example of a non-alcoholic beverage which may have been ordered for its rejuvenating qualities. SARSAPARILLA is native to America and the beverage is derived from the woody vine of the plant. The plant was, and still is, believed to help with respiratory disorders and upset stomach. It was also touted as a remedy for skin and blood problems. It has a flavor similar to root beer. It was popular in the old west and characters in many Westerns have been known to order it instead of whiskey or beer.

5. BOSTON COOLER

1 Lemon Rind in large Bar glass.

3 lumps Ice.

1 bottle Ginger Ale.

1 bottle Sarsaparilla.

Serve.

◇◇◇◇◇◇◇◇◇◇◇◇◇◇◇◇◇◇◇◇◇◇◇◇◇◇◇◇◇◇

Another non-alcoholic beverage, this one with beneficial ginger ale and sarsaparilla. It is recommended that all-natural crafted sodas be used to enjoy the full flavor of the cocktail.

◇◇◇◇◇◇◇◇◇◇◇◇◇◇◇◇◇◇◇◇◇◇◇◇◇◇◇◇◇◇

6. G.O.P.

Use a large Mixing glass with Lump of Ice.

2 jiggers of Orange Juice.
2 jiggers of Grape Fruit Juice.
Fill with Seltzer Water.

Stir; ornament with Fruit and serve with Straws.

◇◇◇◇◇◇◇◇◇◇◇◇◇◇◇◇◇◇◇◇◇◇◇◇◇◇◇◇◇◇◇◇◇◇◇◇◇◇◇

Grapefruit is a relatively recent (1700's) hybrid of an orange and a pomelo. Even though acidic, once digested, grapefruit has an alkaline effect on the body, countering the acidity of our modern diet. The pectin in grapefruit reduces arterial deposits and its vitamin C helps to maintain the elasticity of arteries. The bioflavonoids in grapefruit halt cancer cells from spreading by clearing the body of excess estrogen. Moreover, naringenin, which causes grapefruit's bitter taste, stimulates DNA repair and protects the body from developing cancer. Naringenin has also been found to prevent the formation of kidney cysts. Half of one grapefruit provides over 75% of the recommended daily intake of Vitamin C. It boosts the immune system, relieves sore throats and lessens coughing. Grapefruit aids the digestive process, cleanses the liver and helps to reduce the liver's production of cholesterol. It also helps fight gum disease. Most of these health benefits were probably unknown to those before Prohibition, though they likely did know firsthand that grapefruit juice is invigorating and its aroma reduces stress. The G.O.P. cocktail seems like a great way to start or end the day!

◇◇◇◇◇◇◇◇◇◇◇◇◇◇◇◇◇◇◇◇◇◇◇◇◇◇◇◇◇◇◇◇◇◇◇◇◇◇◇

7. GOLFER'S DELIGHT
Home of Bevo—18th Hole.

Use a large glass Pitcher; fill with Lump Ice.

2 bottles Bevo.

2 bottles Sweet Soda.

Stir well and serve in a Beer glass. Fifty-fifty.

BEVO is the reason the Anheuser-Busch company survived Prohibition. Seeing the writing on the wall, Anheuser-Busch started producing the non-alcoholic malt beverage (near beer) in 1916. Once the Volstead Act was passed in 1919, and the 18th Amendment went into effect in 1920, breweries either switched gears or went out of business.

Anheuser-Busch was successful with the non-alcoholic Bevo and they sold more than five million cases of annually in the 1920's. Others were not so fortunate. Before Prohibition there were thousands of small, hand-crafted breweries in the United States. After Prohibition, the entire industry struggled for decades to the extent that in the 1980's there were fewer than 100 breweries left. In the 1990's interest in the micro-brew renewed. Today the industry has recovered and there are more micro-breweries than ever. Bevo is no longer available so substitute with any non-alcoholic beer of choice.

8. LEMONADE APOLLINARIS
(or Carbonated Water)

Fill large Mixing glass 2/3 full fine Ice.

1 tablespoonful Bar Sugar.

Juice of 1 Lemon.

Fill up with Apollinaris or suitable Carbonated Water. Stir; strain into Lemonade glass; dress with Fruit and serve.

9. SAMTON COCKTAIL

Use a large Mixing glass with Cracked Ice.

1 jigger Orange Juice.

1 jigger imported Ginger Ale.

Fifty-fifty.

Shake well; strain into Cocktail glass and serve.

Non-Alcoholic Cocktail Recipes with Egg

1. BOMBAY COCKTAIL

Use a Claret glass.

½ pony Olive Oil.

½ pony Vinegar.

½ pony Worcestershire Sauce.

Break one Ice Cold Egg into glass.

Add salt and Spanish Paprika and serve.

This is an example of a non-alcoholic cocktail ordered for its nutritional and healthful qualities. The drinkers of the day probably did not know all of the benefits of these ingredients, only that they made them feel better. Today we know that olive oil is a powerful anti-inflammatory and anti-biotic, as well as a healthy source of Omega fats. Vinegar is anti-bacterial and helps to lower blood sugar, among its many other wonderful health benefits. The ingredients in Worcestershire Sauce enhance immunity and mood, as well as improve skin and hair. Whole egg, especially farm fresh, have more benefits than I can list here. Eggs are full of essential vitamins, minerals and healthy fats. Even the Paprika adds to the cocktails advantages with Vitamin A, Vitamin E, Carotenoids and Iron.

2. CIDER EGGNOG

Into a large Bar glass break a fresh Egg.

1 teaspoonful Sugar.

4 lumps Cracked Ice.

Fill up with Sweet Cider.

Shake; strain into tall, thin glass and serve with grated Nutmeg on top.

◇◇◇◇◇◇◇◇◇◇◇◇◇◇◇◇◇◇◇◇◇◇◇◇◇◇◇◇◇◇

SWEET CIDER is also known as apple cider and is non-alcoholic. Cider is made from the juice of apples picked early in the season which have a higher acid content and a lower sugar content. Sweet cider is usually either unpasteurized or less clarified than apple juice. This allows for cider to be fermented into hard apple cider. May substitute with apple juice, though the cocktail won't carry the same depth of flavor.

◇◇◇◇◇◇◇◇◇◇◇◇◇◇◇◇◇◇◇◇◇◇◇◇◇◇◇◇◇◇

3. EGG SOUR

Into small Bar glass drop:

3 lumps Ice.

1 tablespoonful Bar Sugar.

1 Egg.

Juice of 1 Lemon.

Shake well; grate Nutmeg on top and serve with Straw.

◇◇

EGG SOUR is another example of a non-alcoholic cocktail made for its health benefits. The wonderful qualities of eggs were briefly mentioned above but deserve more attention here, especially because eggs went through a period of time when they were unjustifiably maligned. Eggs are an amazing, nearly complete, food. One 75 calorie egg contains 5 g of healthy fat, including omega-3 fatty acids, 6 g of protein and 9 essential amino acids. Eggs contain 100% of the body's needed fat soluble vitamins A, D, E and K as well as over 90% of the calcium, iron, phosphorus, zinc, thiamin, folate, vitamin B6 and vitamin B12 we need. They are also rich in carotenoids, selenium, riboflavin, vitamins B2 and B5 as well as other trace nutrients. One egg contains 113 mg of Choline – a very important brain nutrient which is deficient in upwards of 90% of American diets. There are many more health benefits from eating eggs than this brief summary which you can read more at catinhatbooks.com.

Punch Recipes

1. BLACK AND TAN PUNCH
(For party of 10)

1 lb. white Sugar.

Juice of 6 Lemons.

1 quart Guinness Stout.

1 quart Champagne.

Pour into mixture of Lemon Juice and Sugar the Champagne and Stout, ice cold. Serve in Punch glasses dressed with Fruit.

◇◇◇◇◇◇◇◇◇◇◇◇◇◇◇◇◇◇◇◇◇◇◇◇◇◇◇◇◇◇

GUINNESS STOUT originated in Dublin Ireland in the 1700's and is now one of the most recognized beer brands in the world. It sells about 1.8 billion US pints per year. The Irish dry stout is characterized by a burnt flavor and dark color resulting from roasted unmalted barley. Other ingredients are water, roast malt extract, hops, and brewer's yeast. Guinness stout also is known for its thick, creamy head which forms when poured due to being mixed with nitrogen. Even though it has been called a "meal in a glass", it only has 198 calories per pint.

◇◇◇◇◇◇◇◇◇◇◇◇◇◇◇◇◇◇◇◇◇◇◇◇◇◇◇◇◇◇

2. BOMBAY PUNCH
(2½-gallon mixture for 40 people)

Bruise the skins of 6 Lemons with 1 lb. of Bar sugar, then put the Sugar in a Punch bowl.

Add:

1 box Strawberries.

2 Lemons, sliced.

6 Oranges, sliced.

1 Pineapple, cut into small pieces.

1 quart Brandy.

1 quart Sherry Wine.

1 quart Madeira Wine.

Stir well; empty into another bowl in which a block of Clear Ice has been placed and add:

4 quarts of Champagne.

2 quarts Carbonated Water.

Serve into Punch glasses so that each person will have some of the Fruit.

◇◇

MADEIRA WINE is similar to Port, however substitution with Port is not ideal as Port is sweeter and has less developed flavor profile than Madeira wine . It is a fortified Portuguese wine from the Madeira Islands. It ranges from dry to sweet, and can be enjoyed as an aperitif, a dessert, an addition to cocktails or used in cooking.

◇◇

3. BRANDY SHRUB
(2-gallon mixture for 40 people)

Into a large bowl put the Peeled Rinds of 5 Lemons and the Juice of 12 Lemons and add 5 quarts of Brandy. Cover and seal the bowl; set it aside for 6 days. After the 6 days, add 3 quarts of Sherry wine and 6 pounds of Loaf Sugar, which has been dissolved in 1 quart of plain Soda. Strain through a bag and bottle. For parties, serve using a punch bowl or beverage dispenser. Serve over a full glass of cubed ice.

◇◇

LOAF SUGAR was the primary form of sugar sold in the early 20th century. It was made by pouring hot sugar syrup into a mold which was usually in the shape of a cone or a loaf. When the sugar cooled, it was wrapped and packaged for shipping. In the early 20th century this form was preferable because it was easier to handle than granulated sugar. Some sugar producers still make sugar in this form for nostalgic purposes and it is a very common variety in the developing world.

◇◇

4. CENTURY CLUB PUNCH
(for a party of 5)

Fill glass Pitcher ¼ full Cracked Ice.

½ pint Jamaica Rum.
½ pint Santa Cruz Rum.
2½ pints aerated Water.
2½ tablespoonfuls Bar Sugar.

Stir well and serve in Punch glasses.

5. CHAMPAGNE CUP
(2-gallon mixture)

For mixing use a large Punch bowl or other suitable vessel of made of glass.

4 Oranges, sliced.

4 Lemons, sliced.

½ Pineapple, sliced.

½ pint Chartreuse.

½ pint Abricotine.

1 pint Curacoa.

1 pint Cognac Brandy.

1 pint Tokay Wine.

Stir well and allow mixture to stand three hours. Strain into another bowl and add:

3 quarts Champagne.

3 pints Apollinaris Water.

1 large piece of Ice.

Stir well; decorate with Fruit; float slices of Grape Fruit on top and serve in Champagne glasses.

6. CHAMPAGNE PUNCH
(for a party of 6)

Into a glass Pitcher add:

Juice of 1 Lemon

¼ lb. Bar Sugar.

1 jigger Strawberry Syrup.

1 quart bottle Champagne.

Stir with Ladle and drop in:

1 sliced Orange.

3 slices Pineapple.

Decorate with Fruit and serve in Champagne goblets.

7. CLARET CUP
(2-gallon mixture)

Prepare 3 hours before serving. For mixing use a large glass vessel.

6 Oranges, sliced.

3 Lemons, sliced.

2 Pineapples.

2 jiggers Abricontine.

4 jiggers Curacoa.

4 quarts Claret.

3 pints Apollinaris.

Mix well and set aside for three hours. Strain mixture into a punch bowl and add 3 pints of some sparkling Wine, preferably Champagne. Stir gently once or twice, and then add a large block of clear Ice. Decorate the ice with appetizing Fruits and let several slices of Grapefruit float around in the bowl. Serve in Champagne glasses.

8. CLARET PUNCH (5-gallon mixture for a large reception or party of 100 people)

For mixing use a large glass vessel.

4 lbs. Cut Loaf Sugar.

Juice of 25 Lemons.

2 quarts Brandy.

10 quarts Claret.

7 jiggers Chartreuse.

8 quarts Carbonated Water.

Stir well.

Place a large block of Ice in a Punch bowl and fill nearly full with the mixture, adding:

18 Oranges, cut in slices.

1½ cans sliced Pineapples.

Serve from the bowl into Punch glasses with a Ladle, and renew the contents of the bowl from the mixing vessel as needed.

9. CLUB HOUSE PUNCH
(for a party of 20)

Prepare 6 hours before serving. Mix in a large glass vessel.

½ can Peaches.

½ can Pineapples.

3 Oranges, sliced.

3 Lemons, sliced.

3 quarts Sweet Catawba or Tokay.

1 pint Brandy.

1½ jiggers Jamaica Rum.

1 jigger Green Chartreuse.

Chill in refrigerator for 6 hours. Place block of Ice in a punch bowl of sufficient capacity and strain in the mixture from the Mixing vessel. Dress the Ice with Fruit and serve with a Ladle into Punch glasses.

10. COLD RUBY PUNCH
(2½-gallon mixture for 50 people)

4 lbs. Cut Loaf Sugar.

2 quarts Port Wine.

2 quarts Batavia Arrack.

6 quarts green Tea.

Juice of 24 Lemons.

Chill in refrigerator for several hours. Place block of Ice in a punch bowl of sufficient capacity and strain in the mixture from the Mixing vessel. Dress the Ice with Fruit and serve with a Ladle into Punch glasses.

11. COMPANION PUNCH
(2½-gallon mixture for a reception or party of 50 people)

Into a large Punch bowl pour:

1¼ pints Lemon Juice.

2 pints Gum Syrup.

¾ pint Orange Juice.

1¼ pints Brandy.

6 quarts equal parts Sweet and Dry Catawba.

2 quarts Carbonated Water.

When well stirred place large block of Ice in center of bowl; dress the Ice with Fruit and serve with a Ladle into Punch glasses.

12. COUNTRY CLUB PUNCH

Take 1½ lbs. of Cut Loaf Sugar and rub the lumps on the skins of 4 Lemons and 2 Oranges until the Sugar becomes well saturated with the oil from the skins. Then put the Sugar thus prepared into a large glass vessel, and add:

12 Oranges, sliced.

1 Pineapple, sliced.

1 box Strawberries.

2 bottles (quarts) Apollinaris Water.

Stir thoroughly and add:

1 jigger Benedictine.

1 jigger Red Curacoa.

1 jigger Maraschino.

½ jigger Jamaica Rum.

1 quart Brandy.

4 quarts Tokay or Sweet Catawba Wine.

2 quarts Madeira Wine.

4 quarts Chateau Margaux.

Mix well with oak paddle or ladle and strain into another bowl in which has been placed a block of clear ice. Then pour in 6 quarts Champagne. Decorate the Ice with Fruits, Berries, etc. Serve in Punch cups or glasses, dressing each glass with Fruit and Berries from the bowl.

CHATEAU MARGAUX is a highly acclaimed and expensive wine. In the 1700's, Thomas Jefferson lauded the wine during one of his trips to Bordeaux and he held the wine in his collection. A 1787 Chateau Margaux from Jefferson's collection was valued at an exorbitant $500,000 by its owner in 1989. The bottle was broken at a dinner at the Four Seasons Hotel and insurers paid out $225,000, making it the most expensive wine of all time. Today, good vintages sell for hundreds to thousands of dollars, so you may not want to use a Chateau Margaux for a cocktail or punch. However Chateau Margaux went through a period of time when it was far more affordable and that included the early 1900's pre-Prohibition era. While the wine would impress guests, it probably wouldn't bust your pocket book to pour 4 quarts of Chateau Margaux into a punch bowl. In the late 1800's the Phyloxera pest had attacked the vines of the Margaux village severely harming the region's wine industry. The French vineyards were only saved by grafting the vines onto more robust American rootstock, but harvests were below norm until the 1890's. It took some time after that before the quality of the grape fully returned. While the vineyards survived the World Wars, it wasn't until the 1970's that Chateau Margaux again rose to the international acclaim it enjoys today. Unless your bank account allows for you to pour about $2000 into a punch bowl, you'll have to substitute Chateau Marguax for another full-bodied red.

13. CRIMEAN CUP A LA MARMORA
(for a party of 10)

Into a small Punch bowl pour:

1 pint Orgeat Syrup.

2 jiggers Jamaica Rum.

2 jiggers Maraschino.

2½ jiggers Brandy.

2 tablespoonfuls Bar Sugar.

1 quart Champagne.

1 quart Plain Soda.

Stir well and chill. When cold serve in fancy Stem glasses.

14. EGGNOG
(bowl of 3 gallons)

In a large punch bowl, beat the yolks of 20 Eggs until thin. Stir in 2½ lbs. Bar Sugar until Sugar is thoroughly dissolved. Into this mixture pour:

1½ pints Jamaica Rum.

2 quarts old Brandy.

Mix the ingredients well by stirring. Then pour in the milk (about 2 gallons) slowly, stirring all the while to prevent curdling. Beat the egg whites to a stiff froth and pour carefully over the top of the mixture. Fill Punch glasses from the bowl with ladle and sprinkle a little Nutmeg over each glassful.

15. FISH CLUB PUNCH
(for a party of 8)

Into a Punch bowl pour:

2½ jiggers Lemon Juice.

4 jiggers Peach Brandy.

2 jiggers Cognac Brandy.

2 jiggers Jamaica Rum.

3 pints Ice Water.

Stir well; ladle into Punch glass and serve.

16. GARDEN PUNCH
(2½ gallon mixture for a party of 50)

Place a good size block of Ice in a large Punch bowl.

4 jiggers Lemon Juice.

1½ lbs. Bar Sugar.

2 jiggers Orange Juice.

1½ jiggers green Chartreuse.

1 quart Brandy.

6 Quarts Tokay or Sweet Catawba Wine.

2 quarts Claret Wine.

Stir well; ladle into Stem glasses, and decorate each glass with Fruit before serving.

17. LADIES' DELIGHT
Thursday Luncheon Punch

1 quart of Orange Pekoe Tea (cold).

1 quart of Old Country Club Brandy.

1 pint of Lemon Juice.

1 pint of Orange Juice.

½ pint of Pineapple Juice.

2 quarts Berncastler Berg.

1 pint of Bar Sugar.

Use a large Punch bowl with one Lump of Ice. Pour in mixture; add one quart of Cook's Imperial Champagne. Stir well; decorate with fresh Mint, Fruit in season, and serve.

◇◇

BERNCASTLER BERG refers to wine from the Bernkastel-Kues region of Rhineland-Palatinate, Germany (far west, middle Germany). Winegrowing has been the areas primary industry for centuries. Wines of the region are named for region and winery rather than varietal. Historically Riesling was the most common grape variety grown, as it could withstand the cold winters, short growing season and steep slopes. With the trend toward warmer weather, more varieties are being grown today by the wineries in Bernkastel-Kues. Would be safe to substitute with Riesling.

◇◇

18. PINEAPPLE JULEP
(for a party of 6—Use a small punch bowl)

1 quart of Sparkling Moselle.

1 jigger Cusenier Grenadine.

1 jigger Maraschino.

1 jigger Sir Robert Burnette's Old Tom Gin.

1 jigger Lemon Juice.

1 jigger Orange Bitters.

1 jigger Angostura Bitters.

4 Oranges, sliced.

2 Lemons, sliced.

1 ripe Pineapple, sliced and quartered.

4 tablespoonfuls Sugar.

1 bottle Apollinaris Water.

Place large square of Ice in bowl; dress with the Fruits and serve Julep in fancy Stem glass.

◇◇◇◇◇◇◇◇◇◇◇◇◇◇◇◇◇◇◇◇◇◇◇◇◇◇◇◇◇◇◇◇◇◇◇◇◇◇

SPARKLING MOSELLE is a white sparkling wine produced from wineries along the Moselle River in France, Luxembourg and Germany, which is among the coldest vineyard climates in winemaking. Substitution with another sparkling white would certainly be acceptable to fill out this punch recipe.

◇◇◇◇◇◇◇◇◇◇◇◇◇◇◇◇◇◇◇◇◇◇◇◇◇◇◇◇◇◇◇◇◇◇◇◇◇◇

19. PUNCH A LA ROMAINE
(for a party of 16)

1 bottle Champagne.

1 bottle Rum.

2 tablespoons Dr. Siegert's genuine Angostura Bitters.

10 Lemons.

3 sweet Oranges.

2 pounds Powdered Sugar.

10 fresh Eggs.

Dissolve the Sugar in the Juice of the Lemons and Oranges adding the Rind of 1 Orange.

Strain through a Sieve into a bowl and add by degrees the whites of the Eggs beaten to a froth.

Place the bowl on Ice till cold, then stir in the Rum and Wine until thoroughly mixed. Serve in fancy Stem glasses.

DR. SIEGERT'S GENUINE ANGOSTURA BITTERS still exists today distributed under the company name "Angostura". Dr. Siegert began making bitters in Angostura, Venezula in 1824. In 1875 the family moved the company to Trinidad where is still operates to this day. Angostura now offers 4 varieties of bitters: the original 1824 recipe aromatic bitters, lemon lime bitters, orange bitters and Amaro, which is a combination of the original aromatic bitters, neutral spirits and more spices. The company also offers specialty Rums and Liqueurs.

20. TOKAY PUNCH
(uses 6 pounds of Tokay grapes)

Make a boiling Syrup with three pounds of Sugar and one quart of boiling Water. Pour this mixture over five pounds of Tokay Grapes. When cooled sufficiently, rub the grape mixture through a sieve, leaving skins and seeds behind. Add to the strained grapes the Juice of two Oranges and two Lemons. Add one quart of St. Julien Claret and 1 jigger of Angostura Bitters. Strain mixture and freeze.

Before serving, place frozen mixture in a punch bowl and add 1 pint of good Brandy and one pound of Tokay Grapes. Top with an Italian Meringue Paste of six Egg whites, colored a nice red (optional).

◇◇◇

Tokay wine was called for in several of the above recipes but the wine has no direct relation to TOKAY GRAPES. Also called "Flame Tokay", Tokay grapes are a light red California table grape with a thick skin and seeds. They are available from August through December and have a sweet taste and crisp texture. They have become less popular due to the later developed seedless Flame grapes, though Flames are less sweet than Tokay grapes. The grape was first planted in Lodi, California in 1847 and was thought to get its name from the Hungarian wine Tokay, even though the Tokey dessert wine is made from furmint grapes. For this punch, pick the sweetest, round table grapes available.

◇◇◇

Photo Credits

Page 9. By Orange County Archives [CC BY 2.0 (http://creativecommons.org/licenses/by/2.0)], via Wikimedia Commons

Page 10. 1933 alcohol prohibition ends https://www.flickr.com/photos/77917153@N00/8247541093

Page 11. http://depositphotos.com/12299908

Page 13. http://depositphotos.com/99113882

Page 14. http://depositphotos.com/61966087, http://depositphotos.com/61966099

Page 15. http://depositphotos.com/29983283, http://depositphotos.com/71131627

Page 16. http://depositphotos.com/51137355, http://depositphotos.com/11377355

Page 17. http://depositphotos.com/13429515

Page 19. http://depositphotos.com/80969170

Page 21. By La Correspondencia de España [Public domain], via Wikimedia Commons https://commons.wikimedia.org/wiki/File:1886-liquor-Benedictine.jpg

Page 22. By loki11 (L'Illustration) [Public domain], via Wikimedia Commons https://upload.wikimedia.org/wikipedia/commons/a/a4/Charteuse.jpg

Page 23. By unknown (no credits) (L'Illustration, n° 4214, 8 décembre 1923, p. 27) [Public domain], via Wikimedia Commons https://upload.wikimedia.org/wikipedia/commons/1/12/Cusenier-1923.jpg

Page 24. By unknown (no credits) (L'Illustration, n° 4207, 20 octobre 1923, p. 16) [Public domain], via Wikimedia Commons https://upload.wikimedia.org/wikipedia/commons/0/07/Cherry-Rocher-1923.jpg

Page 25. http://depositphotos.com/12287200

Page 28. http://depositphotos.com/8415600

Page 29. Absinthe Paul Beucler Collection personnelle photo arnold.p ; oct 2007 https://upload.wikimedia.org/wikipedia/commons/6/63/Absinthe_Beucler.jpg

Page 30. http://depositphotos.com/1639203

Page 32. http://depositphotos.com/10633637

Page 33. http://depositphotos.com/13759220

Page 34. http://depositphotos.com/25503105

Page 37. http://depositphotos.com/86413566

Page 38. http://depositphotos.com/12301688

Page 39. By unknown (no credits) (L'Illustration, n° 4212, 24 novembre 1923, p. 25) [Public domain], via Wikimedia Commons https://commons.wikimedia.org/wiki/File:B%C3%A9n%C3%A9dictine-1923.jpg

Page 40. http://depositphotos.com/65126441

Page 41. Jack Delano [Public domain], via Wikimedia Commons https://commons.wikimedia.org/wiki/File:Government_house_rum.jpg

Page 43. http://depositphotos.com/82898430

Page 45. http://depositphotos.com/7358844

Page 46. William James [Public domain or Public domain], via Wikimedia Commons https://commons.wikimedia.org/wiki/File:Five_bartenders_behind_St._Charles_Hotel_bar.jpg

Page 47. http://depositphotos.com/82898370

Page 49. http://depositphotos.com/12680166

Page 50. http://depositphotos.com/75494159

Page 51. http://depositphotos.com/12299595

Page 53. http://depositphotos.com/12299427

Page 54. http://depositphotos.com/12289386

Page 56. By Naotake Murayama (Flickr: These California Wines are All... So Good.) [CC BY 2.0 (http://creativecommons.org/licenses/by/2.0)], via Wikimedia Commons

Page 58. http://depositphotos.com/12301693

Page 59. http://depositphotos.com/61929713

Page 61. http://depositphotos.com/87918748

Page 62. http://depositphotos.com/8563844

Page 64. http://depositphotos.com/11289028

Page 66. http://depositphotos.com/13429022

Page 67. http://depositphotos.com/12287196

Page 69. http://depositphotos.com/39213893

Page 70. http://depositphotos.com/44963315

Page 73. http://depositphotos.com/12298074

Page 75. http://depositphotos.com/12290595

Page 77. http://depositphotos.com/12290209

Page 79. http://depositphotos.com/69022933

Page 80. http://depositphotos.com/32934135

Page 82. http://depositphotos.com/3277940

Page 83. http://depositphotos.com/89280014

Page 85. http://depositphotos.com/57714629

Page 86. http://depositphotos.com/12298451

Page 88. By scanned & uploaded - parkerdr (PHoto section from a scanned post card, dated 1905) [Public domain], via Wikimedia Commons

Page 90. http://depositphotos.com/95260990

Page 92. http://depositphotos.com/90745574

Page 95. http://depositphotos.com/42117073

Page 96. http://depositphotos.com/12289392

Page 97. By Jesus Solana [CC BY 2.0 (http://creativecommons.org/licenses/by/2.0)], via Wikimedia Commons

Page 99. http://depositphotos.com/100075034

Page 100. http://depositphotos.com/24600627

Page 101. http://depositphotos.com/68110125

Page 103. http://depositphotos.com/99114554

Page 104. http://depositphotos.com/10670725

Page 107. http://depositphotos.com/98093426

Page 109. http://depositphotos.com/86444062

Page 110. http://depositphotos.com/57715187

Page 112. http://depositphotos.com/12291641

Page 114. http://depositphotos.com/13429022

Page 118. By advertisment, edited and primarily uploaded by https://en.wikipedia.org/wiki/User:JonathanDavidArndt [CC BY-SA 3.0 (http://creativecommons.org/licenses/by-sa/3.0)], via Wikimedia Commons

Page 120. By Canada Dry [Public domain or Public domain], via Wikimedia Commons

Page 122. By Piaget - van Ravenswaay [Public domain], via Wikimedia Commons

Page 126. http://depositphotos.com/5048906

Page 127. http://depositphotos.com/29192055, http://depositphotos.com/9593282

Page 130. http://depositphotos.com/12287211

Page 132. http://depositphotos.com/4306790

Page 133. http://depositphotos.com/12291249

Page 135. http://depositphotos.com/12287214

Page 136. http://depositphotos.com/12299539

Page 138. http://depositphotos.com/12291439

Page 140. http://depositphotos.com/13297391

Page 141. http://depositphotos.com/82901268

Page 142. http://depositphotos.com/82900504

Page 144. By Sketch by W. Voigt [Public domain], via Wikimedia Commons

Page 145. http://depositphotos.com/17613121

Page 146. By Giulio Marguglio (18 Isolabella) [CC BY-SA 2.0 (http://creativecommons.org/licenses/by-sa/2.0)], via Wikimedia Commons

Made in the USA
Las Vegas, NV
06 December 2023